THE RELUCTANT HOTELKEEPER

THE RELUCTANT HOTELKEEPER

A Memoir

John Searancke

Matador
9 Priory Business Park,
Wistow Road, Kibworth Beauchamp,
Leicestershire. LE8 0RX
Tel: 0116 279 2299
Email: books@troubador.co.uk
Web: www.troubador.co.uk/matador
Twitter: @matadorbooks

ISBN 978 1789017 571

British Library Cataloguing in Publication Data.
A catalogue record for this book is available from the British Library.

Typeset in 12pt Adobe Caslon Pro by Troubador Publishing Ltd, Leicester, UK

Matador is an imprint of Troubador Publishing Ltd

For my late mother-in-law, Joan Emily Boughton
1920 – 2017
With much love

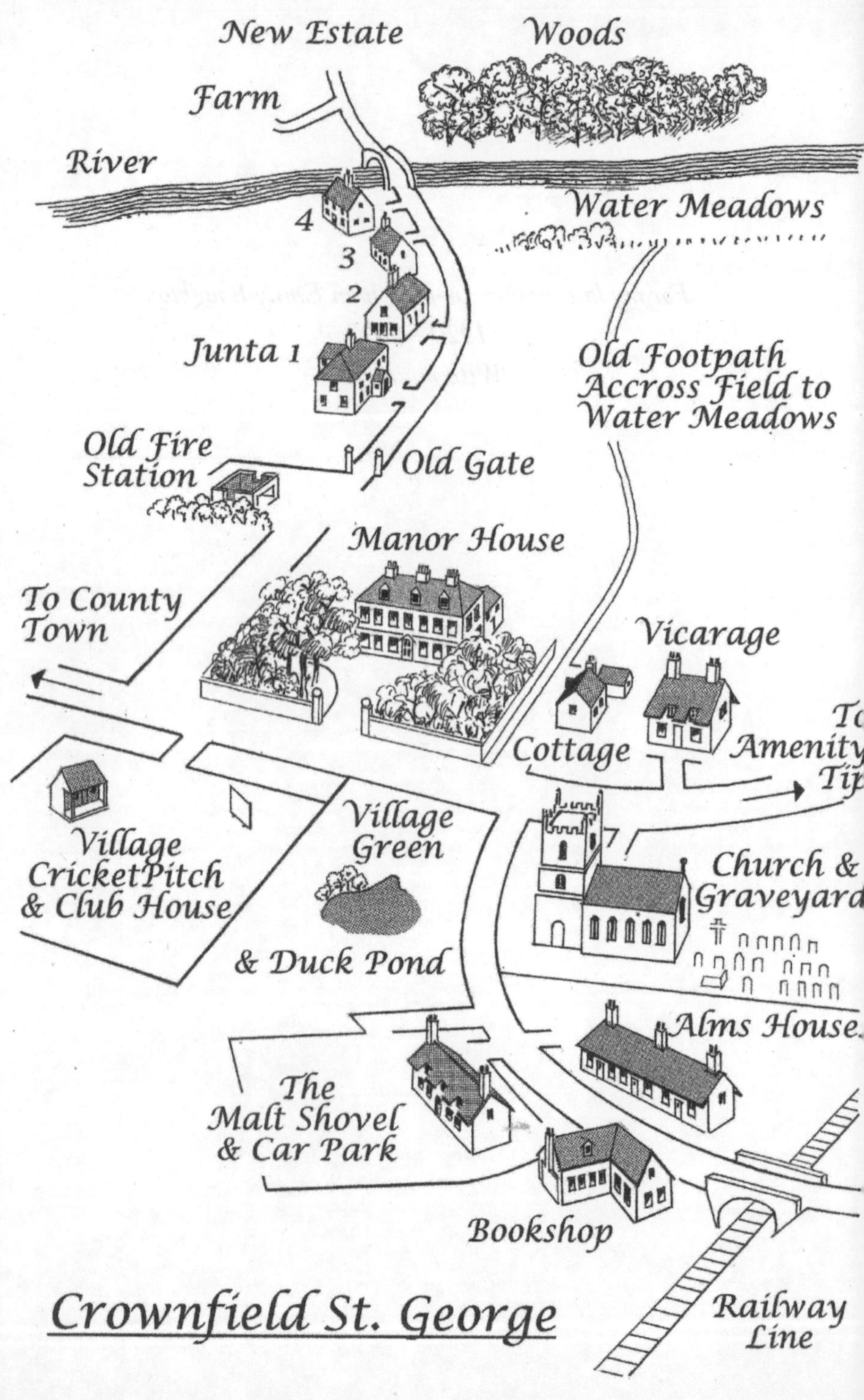
New Estate
Woods
Farm
River
4
3
2
Junta 1
Water Meadows
Old Footpath
Accross Field to
Water Meadows
Old Fire
Station
Old Gate
Manor House
To County
Town
Vicarage
Cottage
Amenit
Village
Green
7
Church &
Graveyar
Village
CricketPitch
& Club House
& Duck Pond
Alms House
The
Malt Shovel
& Car Park
Bookshop
Crownfield St. George
Railway
Line

CONTENTS

ABOUT THE AUTHOR

John Searancke was born in 1943 at Derby Royal Infirmary, and thus a war baby. He lived his early life in Ashby-de-la-Zouch, a market town in Leicestershire, and was sent away to be educated at Kings Mead Preparatory School, Seaford and afterwards at Rugby School. Later commissioned into the Territorial Army, he has been variously an hotel and restaurant owner, director and chairman of a marketing consortium, and latterly a partner with his wife in a commercial legal services company. He has enjoyed his working life in England and Switzerland and now lives with his wife Sally in West Sussex and northern Tenerife, where for five years he occupied himself as restaurant critic for a Canarian newspaper.

His first book, ***Dog Days in The Fortunate Islands***, the stories of moving his family and dog to live on a small island in the Atlantic Ocean received much acclaim. It is available in paperback and e-book formats.

Prunes for Breakfast is his second book and records the life and times of his father throughout WW2, including a cache of unpublished personal letters with details of his landing in Normandy, fighting through the *bocage* and later capture and incarceration in a German POW Camp. It is available in paperback, e-book and audio formats.

The Reluctant Hotelkeeper is his third book and forms a prequel to ***Dog Days in The Fortunate Islands***. It is available in paperback and e-book formats.

Please visit the website for information about all books and more.

www.johnsearancke.com

Prologue

All was confusion, total confusion.

The hotel was open for business, but there was no longer anyone at the helm. The ship was rudderless, save for Carol, the long-serving and trusted manager. Staff were itching to get on with things, anything at all, but lacked direction. The new owners did not know what was expected of them and were too stubborn to ask for my help or advice on their first day, as I, the outgoing owner, stood by watching and ready to leave. There was an impasse, and so a state of paralysis ruled over the entire hotel. Then, to cap it all, guests started to arrive for their weekend away, as guests tend to do, completely unaware of the change of ownership.

Strictly speaking, Sally and I should do nothing; it was no business of ours anymore. But a quick glance from me to Carol, an almost imperceptible nod in return, and things clicked back into action. Orders were briskly given, actions undertaken, and those guests, the very first since the sale of the business, were checked in and went to their room blissfully unaware of the upheaval all around them.

The new owners stood glowering in my direction. They had point blank refused our aid and so there was no more that we could do. I went over to Carol and shook her hand, wishing her luck. Then I hugged her close and whispered in her ear:

"You can make this work. I know that you can do it. I am really going to miss you. Thank you so much for everything…"

Over thirty-five years or so my team and I had changed a run-down, semi-derelict building to a respected country house hotel, garnering along the way a clutch of industry awards that made us the envy of our competitors. I had toiled night and day to make my vision come true, putting in the hours each week that would have been quite illegal in the public domain should I have been a member of a trade union. No, it was never easy, of course, not one single step. Thirty-five hard-fought years, and that chapter of my life was no more.

Sally took the hint and faded away around the side of the building, to reappear a minute later as she brought the car round to the front door, and I jumped in. As if on military parade, the entire staff of the hotel lined up on the steps, wearing their best uniforms, to wave us on our way. I waved back quickly and we pulled out of the driveway and towards the main road before anyone other than Sally could see the tears in my eyes.

Chapter 1

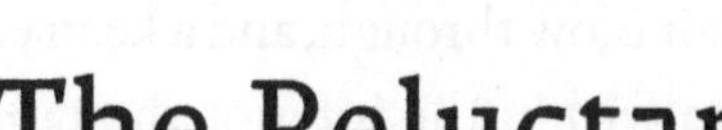

The Reluctant Hotelkeeper

The elegant and perfectly proportioned Queen Anne building shimmered in the heat haze of an English summer's afternoon in early August. Clad down one side by a beautiful old creeping white wisteria, its boughs gnarled and twisted through the years, the flowery fronds cascading down like a waterfall, there was little to give away the fact that this was a country house hotel other than for a discreet plaque by the front gates. Old, faded russet-coloured brickwork complemented by cream painted wooden sash windows below the tiled roof created a picture postcard image of the English country house. But inside that outer shell, it hummed with the urgent need to make the graceful old building work to pay its way.

Now, in the middle of that idyllic summer afternoon, all was quiet, save for the occasional buzz of hovering bumblebees as they sought pollen from the adjacent beds of lavender. No cars were to be seen on the sweep of gravelled driveway to mar the perfect symmetry, nor on the adjacent car parking area, neatly screened from casual view by a row of low bushes, clipped into a perfect straight line like a row of evergreen soldiers forever standing to attention.

The tall oak front door to the hotel lay wide open, letting the warm air blow through, and a keen ear might just discern from deep within the interior the tapping of keys on an aged typewriter as Carol, the long-suffering hotel manager, caught up with the pile of brochure requests left in a neat heap for her attention. This was a daily chore, but the sending out of the new colour brochure, accompanied by a personalised letter, was surely to be the lifeblood of this business.

From across the great field opposite could be heard the distant calling to heel of a couple of dogs, prior to them being ushered in through the front door a few minutes later. A small sigh escaped from Carol's lips as she realised that her quiet afternoon's peace was probably about to be shattered. Looking up over the old mahogany reception desk, she saw me, now the owner of the hotel, and greeted me with her usual ready and engaging smile.

"Hi. Don't worry, Carol. I've just popped in to say that I'm back. I'll see you at six as usual."

"No problem, everything is under control. Hi, Moss, hi Midge." That latter part was addressed to my dogs. As keen on dogs as I, she never failed to make a fuss of them.

Always smartly turned out and on time for her shifts, Carol was a great asset to the hotel. She had arrived in response to a local advertisement and fitted in well as a receptionist and general dogsbody, as one has to do in a small hotel. Initiative and willingness brought her to the fore, and now she was manager, taking great swathes of burden from my shoulders. She had become truly indispensable, and I hope that she realised how highly I valued her, way above any other member of staff. Through thick and thin, she was there for me.

I ambled back out through the front door, trailing the Border terriers in my wake, and walked across the lane to my small get-away-from-it-all cottage. There would be just enough time to put my feet up and have a refreshing cup of tea before facing the barrage of often pointless or inane questions from my more eccentric customers. How come I seemed to get all the dotty ones? What had I done to have more than my fair share? And more to the point, just why had I got myself here in the first place?

Crownfield St. George: the name conjured up everything that one might desire of a sleepy and quintessentially English country village with a couple of pubs, a church at the top of the hill, a slightly overgrown cricket ground and, of course, a village green complete with murky pond, all overlooked rather proprietorially by the old Manor House, now a semi-functioning hotel of sorts in the making. Images of the crack of leather on willow, making hay in the summer sunshine, and a pace of life long forgotten were conjured back to mind as one passed along the narrow, winding road through the village.

I had first arrived there in the middle '60s and I confess to having known absolutely nothing about the running of an hotel, so how had I got myself involved in this business? Well, my parents had bought the achingly elegant but ramshackle old place when, unbeknownst to me, their marriage was quietly foundering and they were on the cusp of splitting up. Quite why either of them had thought that buying and running an hotel out in the countryside would be a good thing to do to save their marriage is something that will forever escape me, as it is too late now to ask them.

My father had sold his family business, a building company up in the Midlands where I had grown up and was presently living and working in my first job, and bought this place further south, presumably thinking that it would be something to occupy my mother. His ever-active brain had stood him in good stead throughout his service during the last war and then in the years thereafter when the building industry picked up so dramatically with the replacement of national housing stock. On the rare occasions that my father and I met then, because we just didn't get on, he seemed to have become almost aimless with insufficient to occupy him. Instead, as far as I could see, he resorted to taking himself off to the nearby golf course at every opportunity, returning much later, occasionally somewhat the worse for wear.

How my long-suffering mother coped with all that, I do not know. She was the daughter of a well-to-do Derbyshire family with their own solicitors' practice in Ripley, on the edge of the glorious Peak District. I imagined that she had wanted for almost nothing, with family servants and a motor car, and had never needed to do a day's work in her life other than as a wife and then a mother. Tall, slim and straight of back, she was always clad in either a twin-set of sweater and cardigan, or, should she be going out, a more formal two-piece suit, with low heels, and finally crowned by a soft perm to her fine pale hair. A very serious motor accident (no fault of her own) had resulted in her being fitted with a plastic replacement hip, and left with a limp. She leaned occasionally on a walking stick, whilst pretending that she really had no need of it. The surgeons had told her that she might never walk again after the crash, but she was determined to prove them wrong – and so she jolly well did. She was a living and graceful relic of a bygone era, and nothing wrong with that, in my opinion.

But she and my father could not have been more like chalk and cheese, he being more down to earth and a little overweight from latterly enjoying the good things of life. One could forgive him that, I suppose, when the time he had spent in a German prisoner of war camp after the Normandy landings in World War Two was taken into account.

Perhaps it was because my father had owned a building company that he felt that this old hotel, which was in need of major modernisation, could be one last challenge – a wonderful conversion back to its glory days, his swan song towards retirement? Cooped up in close proximity to his wife throughout the working day whilst improvements were being made, however, was always going to be a disaster for a person like my father.

When they first bought the hotel, the senior member of staff was a Scottish lady spinster in charge of the kitchen. Her name was Miss Brown, and I cannot recall anyone who ever called her anything other than that. I always assumed that she had been born without a forename. She ran the kitchen with a rod of iron and I, like everyone else, was terrified of her. I cannot recall passing more than a few words with her.

"Here is the lunch menu." She placed it neatly on the edge of the desk in the office, before turning about and retiring.

"Thank you, Miss Brown."

A nod, and she was gone.

How menus evolved was a complete mystery to me. Does anyone remember Brown Windsor soup? I found it to be quite palatable, as with Mock Turtle soup. Her choice of menu having appeared in the office, the hotel secretary would duplicate it on one of those ancient Gestetner machines, cranking a handle to produce the required number of often blurred copies.

When Miss Brown was ready to serve, a large gong would be sounded in the hall. Whether for luncheon (as it then was), or for dinner, 1p.m. or 7p.m. on the dot, the result was always the same. There was a stampede – albeit a rather refined one. Ladies would put down their glass of sherry, brush down their dresses (never trousers!) and gentlemen would fiddle with their cravats and shoot their cuffs. Some even preened their waxed moustaches, the better perhaps to keep them from trailing into the Brown Windsor soup. When all were seated, then the soup would be brought out from the kitchen and ladled into bowls. If you had only just arrived as a guest, you might not have understood the meaning of that gong. Latecomers simply missed the soup course.

Sadly, Miss Brown was not to last very long, before a fire destroyed her accommodation and her entire kitchen, although fortunately she did not herself go up in flames. Quite soon after my parents purchased the lovely old house, someone managed to set fire to the outbuildings which were designated for future development to improve the staff quarters and perhaps to create further guest rooms. There was a strong rumour, nay more than just a rumour, a suspicion as to how the conflagration had occurred, and it included a tasty tale, not entirely apocryphal, about a live-in chambermaid, candles and midnight trysts with a lusty local yokel. But that perhaps is a story for another time.

The fire engines from the next town arrived too late to extinguish the blaze and were further hampered by the fact that the hydrant near to the main road had been artfully concealed by a large lorry load of grit, carefully and stupidly placed there by the local council many moons previously, to throw over any areas of black ice that might develop in winter and to assist with traction on the nearby hill. In any case, I imagined the conversation between the firefighters along the following lines, and I hope that I don't malign them:

"Bob, where's the bloody hydrant then?"

"Dunno. It's marked on the plan as being over there, innit."

"Well, go and check it out, mate, and pronto. Otherwise the whole place is going to go up."

"The only place that it can be is right under that huge pile of winter road grit!"

"Bugger that! We can't possibly shift all that lot before the whole place has gone."

"Ring the council…?"

"Don't be daft. There will be nobody there at this time of night."

"Oh well then, not much we can do, is there…"

"Best light up another fag then and let's have a brew."

And that was the end of those outbuildings, a smouldering pile of rubble the only remains. Part of my parents' new dream had just gone up in smoke.

I have no memories of my early childhood or teenage years other than in the context of schooling, and boarding school at that. An only child, I came from parents "of the old school". My mother would have enjoyed a life of ease with the use of servants around her until she met and married my father. I was bundled off to Preparatory School at the tender age of seven. That school could not have been located at a greater geographical distance, right down on the South Coast, had they planned it! Perhaps they did?

I was put on to the school train at London Victoria where a master would sign me in, check that my trunk was safely stowed on board with a hundred or so others and then place me into one of the reserved seats. An unenviable task, but woe betide that I should move to sit with a friend further along the carriage. At half term, there would be a brief break which, in my case, was spent with my parents at the Queens Hotel in Brighton and, more often than not, either sampling the many delights of the West Pier or going for a ride on the famous Volks Electric Railway that ran along the seafront towards Rottingdean.

My father, a distant figure, perhaps even lonely, had spent a year in a German POW Camp after his capture in Normandy soon after the landings there. He wrote home positively from the camp, but many people have recorded how life there could change a man. Certainly, he remained remote from me.

My recall of early teenage years is fractured, to say the least. I do remember, though, going to the Isle of Man virtually every summer holiday. Father would be absent on the golf course all day, and then in the evening he was an aloof figure presiding over our dinner table in the hotel restaurant. Were we on the island because that was where he had passed through OCTU, the military officer training school?

Another memory is of my first proper bicycle; a maroon coloured Raleigh with horrid whitewall tyres. I was thoroughly castigated when, one day, I went out to ride it. My father, who was at home for some reason, had ignored me so I just took off and went for a spin, needing to get away from things.

Apoplectic with anger on my return, crimson of cheek and with spittle flying, he demanded "Where have you been?"

"Just out." I said with a small shrug. My monosyllabic response clearly riled him.

"But where did you go?" Anger was getting the better of him.

"Nowhere..."

I tried to explain that I had literally cycled aimlessly around the local area for about an hour, as I suspect many young boys did, but it was an alien concept to him, and our relationship faltered anew. It was actually a relief to get back to Rugby, a great public school that my father had entered me down for at birth – probably at the same time as he wrote to Mr Ford from his POW Camp and ordered a new car. Yes, truly, he did.

I went my own way after leaving Rugby and do not recall seeing my parents for some while. It came as a major shock to find that they had cut their ties with Ashby-de-la-Zouch, moved house, and decamped further south. How did one's parents come to decide on moving house, selling a long-established family business and then literally doing the move, all without their son being aware in the slightest of what was going on?

And now here I was, returning back into the family fold. Who was the mad one here?

"Err...might you...?"

The sentence drizzled away to nothing and the silence became all-pervading down the line. Who would break that silence first? My mother, bless her, was not so good at asking direct questions; and my father would never have been persuaded to ask me himself. But the message was clear:

Would I move, to go and help, if only for a while? Please...

And so, in an effort to bail my parents out of the disaster that they had created for themselves, I packed my scant belongings into my trusty Ford Allardette and headed further south.

Did I really want to move south, away from my roots and friends? No. Did I really want to work with or for my parents? Again, no. Did I have any skills that I could bring along? No, again. Callow youth that I was, only a few months past my majority and fresh from a job in light engineering that I disliked intensely, I had only a few hundred pounds to my name at the local Westminster Bank, and I reckoned that wouldn't go far. Neither parent was indiscreet enough to offer any remuneration for what I took to be a temporary assignment, so I had to fend for myself. Food was, of course, supplied, and I made sure that my car was filled up regularly as well. As to the rest, well, if there was no money, there was no money.

I had first met Ann, the young lady who was to become my first wife whilst I was still living in the Midlands. She was a photographic model and I thought her to be dazzlingly attractive. She agreed to move further south with me and quickly found a job in a nearby town rather than joining me at the hotel, and that suited both of us just fine. With me was Becket, the Cairn terrier who had come to me as a puppy, bought from a farm near Stratford upon Avon. He had vomited all over the seats of my Allardette on the way back to my digs. We had wonderful times together, Becket on the road with me more often than not and by then happy in the car.

When I answered the clarion call and turned up at the hotel, I pitched in to everything. As far as I can remember, my mother did little else other than to swan around being gracious to the guests – though she actually had a canny brain, she seemed unwilling or unable to apply it to the urgent problems to hand – and my father was seldom seen, having beaten that hasty retreat to the local golf course.

During those early days after my arrival at my parents' new hotel, I was really out of my depth, knowing nothing about the type of business, and knowing nothing either as to how I might extricate us from the enormous hole into which we appeared to be sliding. Many were the times that I thought that I had bitten off more than I could chew, and, in the darkest hours, thought of throwing in the towel. I rued the day that I had agreed to lend a hand.

I was surprised and alarmed to see that there was an hotel secretary. A very pleasant, educated, middle aged lady, I got on quite well with her from the start, but just what did she actually do? She came in each morning for a few hours but appeared to spend far too much of her time chatting with my parents and taking coffee rather than fulfilling any real function. I could not help but think that she was an extravagance for an almost bankrupt hotel. There was really no need for someone to be employed to answer the phone or to type letters on the creaky Underwood, was there? One of us could do all of that without incurring extra outside expenditure, surely. And book-keeping was not a problem either in those days because there was not much of it to do. The accountant had handed me a ledger and I started to fill it in, with separate areas for income and expenditure. But, oh, what a saving the departure of that secretary would make in due course, I thought.

Within a month or two any thoughts on that matter were rendered unnecessary, as she resigned and went to live with and care for her elderly father at the other end of the village. To my utter amazement, another lady promptly took her place, found from nowhere, as far as I knew, and hastily installed by my father. So much for trying to make rather obvious savings.

I learned that the accountants engaged by my father had written stern warnings of impending doom, should not the business turn over a new leaf and find its feet – and pronto. Meanwhile my parents' marriage continued to drift slowly yet further into oblivion – though they must have tried to keep the worst of it from me. I was stunned and mortified when my father finally decamped with that damned replacement hotel secretary – a keen golfer like him. I went one day on my rounds checking bedrooms and walked into one...the rest is better left unrecorded. It was a storyline that could not have been invented, must have shattered my mother, let alone me, and resulted in almost complete estrangement between my father and myself.

It then fell to me to man either the quarterdeck or the lifeboat, whichever way one chose to look at it. I just could not bring myself to jump ship into that lifeboat, even though the urge to do so was so strong. Was it a matter of personal pride? And so, I consigned my reluctance temporarily to the back of a mental cupboard and resolved to take my stand on the quarterdeck and to buckle down and make a good fist of it. Could I do it?

What on earth would it be like to try to run an hotel with my own mother, a figurehead who lived on the premises but had no knowledge of the running of the business, and seemed disinterested to want to do so? Yes, I was hesitant in the extreme but fired up by the challenge of going one better than my father. What a challenge it would turn out to be. Lack of self-confidence, night sweats and the terror of being found out through my ignorance of what was required often reduced me to a quivering wreck, though I strove mightily to conceal it. The differences from my old job could not have been greater. I hated, with a passion which was never to desert me, the overlong hours that were to become my norm. Some days, most days, it took a real effort to leave my bed, knowing that I would be on my feet for fourteen hours or so with nary a break. But, you have to do what you have to do... Why, oh why, is there a common misconception that the life of a hotelkeeper is an easy one?

When I had first came on the scene, the coffers were virtually empty, though the place was trading, albeit at a significant and unsustainable loss. There was no money either to promote or to develop it. Anyway, there was not much to promote at first, it was so decrepit, though potentially so achingly beautiful. The word "marketing" was one that had never crossed the minds of my parents, and nor, to be truthful, had it much entered mine.

And so, I reluctantly undertook the process of drawing up my first strategic plan for the business and putting my fledgling ideas down on paper. It would be sink or swim, and my pride could not contemplate the idea of sinking. When I roughly costed out the long list of what I had deemed to be instant and vital necessities, we could barely afford to do even one of them. How was I to prioritise? What was most important in order to generate revenue? And, since I knew nothing about the business, who was going to say if I was moving in the right direction anyway?

I immediately discovered that there was an extra fixture that had not been on any inventory, if indeed there had been one at all, back in those days – a lovely little old lady by the name of Daisy who seemed to come with the place.

She was lacking most of her teeth and was ancient, wizened and stooped, with the fewest of wisps of hair remaining on top of her head. Always to be seen in a flowery pinafore, she had been there for ever, it appeared, and she resided in what could fairly be described as a large walk-in cupboard. Most to the point, she seemed to have no particular job. She pottered about, was very polite when she spoke – which was seldom – and withdrew each evening to her cupboard, not to be seen again until the following morning, when she took to providing my mother with an early morning cup of tea. Apart from that, we fed and watered her and I really cannot remember anything else that she did. I cannot even remember her going outside the building.

She appeared to have just been inherited with the hotel as part of the inventory. What one should do about that quite flummoxed me. It must have been at least a couple of years before she came one day to see my mother and announced that she was going back to her family in Ireland, and she just upped-sticks and disappeared that afternoon. And that was that.

Another odd employee was Jill. She was a teenaged girl, the daughter of friends of my parents, who hailed from Ashby-de-la-Zouch in Leicestershire. They wanted her to have some experience of life outside of her immediate family and asked if we would take her in. She was with us for about two years, fitting in where needed, and during that time managed to get herself married without either us or her parents knowing anything about it! She had met a chap in a town nearby on her days off, and obviously the relationship had flourished, but I presume that her parents would not have approved from the telephone exchanges between my mother and hers when my mother felt duty bound to reveal the situation to her parents. Conversations between the two were decidedly frosty for some while.

Anyway, Jill came downstairs one morning, worked the breakfast shift but was not to be seen preparing tables for lunchtime. It transpired her room had been cleared out and her belongings mysteriously spirited away without anybody being the wiser. She had disappeared, never to be seen again. We later heard from her parents that she had fetched up in Grimsby, and set up home with her new husband. I don't think that her parents found out more about it for six months or so.

Hotel life was ever to be full of surprises.

I have lost count of the people who have told me over the years that they envied me so much, that it must all be so easy; visualising themselves leaning on the bar and taking shedloads of money, readily handed over in exchange for paltry effort. The reality of life in the hotel business is so very different, and the hours required to make a success of any hotel are punishing. The easiest part of the equation is acquiring your chosen business. After that, the really hard work begins. Why should I expect people to spend their hard-earned money with me rather than elsewhere, keeping me and my business afloat through good times and bad?

Indeed, bad times they were a-coming.

No wonder that I was soon having those second thoughts. I suppose that it is the same for every young person starting out in a new job, but in my case, there was no safety net. What did I know of what had been so suddenly thrust upon my young shoulders?

So, my new life began to take on shape. As soon as I had got my feet under the table properly, I realised that my doubts and reluctance had been well founded. Initially pulled from pillar to post, trying to run with countermanding orders, all I could do was to go with the flow of daily life and try to take comfort from the fact that everything was ripe for change.

Chapter 2

Saved by the Bells

The greatest upheaval of my life was yet to come – the birth of my son, Marcus, my pride and joy. I was soon rushing to the telephone box on the corner outside the cottage hospital to trumpet the news to everyone that I could think of, and probably quite a few who were not interested at all, gabbling sixteen to the dozen no doubt while thrusting a diminishing pile of coppers into the coin payment slot before my minutes ran out.

That time seemed to pass in a blur. I must have been pulling double shifts, both at home and at work for a considerable period of time as Ann took to her full-time mothering role at home. I have little memory of how we all coped, but we seemed to have survived as one must do, particularly in the hotel industry.

We had no money to speak of and my first year at the hotel had resulted in a resounding loss, which our accountant had been at pains to point out would be unsustainable should things continue as they were. The bank manager was even more forthcoming, ominously talking about the status of my newly minted mortgage. I could only agree with him because the position was crystal clear for anyone to see. However, I had to maintain faith in my long-term planning: I was operating an hotel from a delightful building, apart from the dilapidations, lack of facilities, and almost everything else, and I had the confidence (of youth) that it would all come right in the end.

I was desperate for a break, and some good luck for a change, when the proverbial bacon was saved by two very nice retired gentlemen who arrived at the hotel within a few weeks of each other, both accompanied by their respective immediate families, who lived locally.

I was interviewed by someone from each family to see if I might be a suitable candidate to provide them with hotel facilities. They had heard that we were open for business, albeit in our own rather haphazard and unique way. It seems that I passed their interviews, probably because I underquoted them in a desperate effort to gain some business traction.

I had serious reservations (no pun intended) about taking on people who would in effect become permanent residents, but when needs must… I needed those gentlemen's money. It was as simple as that. Each of them signed up to take a room on an open-ended basis. One of them was a quite delightfully spoken and, as I soon discovered, very erudite and cultured gentleman (in the real old-fashioned sense of the word) who owned an aging

VW Beetle, which sported a superb private number plate of one letter and two numbers which I coveted. Even then all those years ago, it must have far exceeded the value of the ancient Beetle. He spent much of his day painting watercolours of the surrounding countryside. He was very good at that and I still have one of his paintings.

The other gentleman, the Commander (RN retired), liked his tipple, and I was very happy to accommodate his regular desire for a large glass of Bells whisky. It was a welcome bonus for our struggling finances, though I never saw him in his cups, despite him starting the process about 11 o'clock in the morning. I celebrated by putting in an order for a case of whisky. The wholesaler was so surprised that he telephoned to ask if it was a mistake, as he was only too well aware that I would normally order a bottle at a time.

Sometime later, another prospective long-term guest hove over the horizon and settled herself on a settee in the lounge. Again, I was interviewed. This time it was a lady – a titled lady, no less – a spinster, and a well-known authoress. She wrote under a pseudonym and spent a number of months with us as she wrote her next book, one of an extensive series of best-selling period romance novels. Her account was always settled on the button each week by a cheque written out by her publishers. She was difficult, very demanding, and blind as a bat without her thick pebble glasses, but rather welcome at that time all the same.

We then had a small but steady income that allowed me to start to promote the hotel. I so disliked self-promotion, for that is what it really is, and I confess, some fifty years later, to still disliking it. But there was to be no escape from the necessity. I tried all sorts of stuff, most of which I learned about by going around other hotels to see what they were doing. Another hotelier that I knew told me such activity is called "competitive analysis" and that the taxman would allow my costs incurred to be set against my non-existent profit. I employed it to the full over the years, visiting all sorts of establishments to pick up hints and tips along the way. Visits to such places, and meals at, were much enjoyed as a business expense. To be fair, though, I learned an awful lot by going to check out better hotels than mine. Tricks of the trade are legion, and I took them all home with me, stored away to be dusted off and brought out when the time was ripe and funds would allow.

Quite definitely nowhere near the top of my list of things to be done was replacement of the hotel china. But you know how it is – I had a personal problem with that china, and it offended me greatly…

I still remember first walking into the old original dining room and being aghast at finding completely mismatched tables – different shapes, different woods, different heights (I could go on) – and odd chairs, with about five different types of random crockery neatly laid out for non-existent lunches or high teas. An older reader might remember those tea sets to be found in old-fashioned village tea shops, either of a light green hue, a yellowish beige, or more daringly, a faded blue. We had all three shades in action, artfully placed on each table by a charming but dim elderly waitress of whom it might be fair to say that she had never crossed the county boundary. It no longer surprised me to know that there were many such people who had never travelled far from their home village, despite the invention of the motor car and steam train.

That crockery; it just had to go, it really did. My mother seemed to gaze blankly over such things and when there was something that she didn't like, she would feign ignorance as though it wasn't there. I had a horror of the stuff every time I saw it. Moreover, there were chips or cracks on most of the cups and saucers. How could you expect people to eat off stuff like that? So, rather adventurously, I hired a van and drove up to the Potteries, in the Stoke on Trent area, where I visited a number of manufacturers and eventually settled on a mid-blue design on a white background that I liked best, from a manufacturer in (I seem to recall) Burslem. I bought directly from the factory at greatly reduced cost. Not expecting a totally truthful reply, I did ask if they had plans to continue that particular line, and the gods must have been with me because it remained in production and saw me happily through the next fifteen years or so. It was my first shot at the concept of long-term strategic planning.

But I had certainly put the cart before the horse. We then had wonderful crockery, but few customers to pay for their usage. The bank paid for it, as it were.

Further emboldened, I then took the decision to remove all of the "gazunders" from the bedrooms. They actually resided within small bedside cabinets, but I was firmly of the opinion that no self-respecting hotel needed to maintain these in nightly usage even in the middle '60s. Overnight, I became a hero – albeit temporarily – to the upstairs staff.

The taking on of new members of staff was not something that I had done before, but I was thrown in at the deep end. Advertisements in the local papers elicited a number of enquiries from local village people with not a lot of relevant skills but a willingness to learn. Speed of movement was of the essence, and that had to be inbuilt from the start. If they ambled about, stopping here and there and then forgetting what they were there for, they would never turn out to be the sort of staff that I needed. You cannot have a slow waiter or waitress, and that goes for most other departments in an hotel too. It was often possible to tell by the way they first came in through the front door. We decided to provide a uniform for them so that got over any lack of dress sense.

One of our first employees was Margaret, a nun. My mother first encountered her in the lane, as they were out walking. Sister Margaret came into the hotel, in her full habit, and quietly suggested that a position as a part-time waitress would suit her.

"Err…would you be wearing what you have got on now?" I was just a bit embarrassed by this whole encounter. It seemed so surreal.

"No, of course not!" She waved her arms around and gave me a wide smile. "Just normal clothes."

"Oh." I couldn't think of what else to say.

"Well then…?"

"How about coming in this evening then? We do have some guests staying, but we aren't busy, so it would be an easy introduction. Come in just before six."

I really almost didn't recognise her. No nun's habit, a dash of makeup and modern clothes. It was quite a transformation, and she took to it like a duck to water.

Later, I walked back up the lane with my dog and chatted to her as we strolled along. She told me that she was on some sort of sabbatical before her final vows and that she would be returning to her Order in about six months, but in the meantime, she was enjoying time with her family and wanted to carry on at the hotel a couple of times a week. I enjoyed the easy relationship immensely, bumping into her along the lane with her wimple flapping in the breeze, and I was so sorry when she left.

The property, many years before it became an hotel, had long been listed as a Grade II building, taking pride of place in the conservation area in the old part of the village. So, an immediate nightmare descended as my first shots at planning applications were summarily thrown out, as were all subsequent modifications.

I was at a bit of a loss to understand because those first applications were all for internal work, which my local architect thought should sail through. All were for the creation of en-suite bathrooms to a number of bedrooms, now becoming a requirement for ever more discerning guests, with English tourists returning from holiday packages at new hotels in Spain where en-suite facilities were fast becoming standard. There was no way that the work could have had any bearing on neighbours, near or far. Being a listed building has always proved to be a two-edged sword, and on balance caused me more problems than it could ever solve.

The neighbours, though relatively distant either up the lane or across the road, took it upon themselves to get together as a small army of vociferous objectors, seeking to take me to task over every point of planning or law – anything to stop development of the hotel into a profitable business. I had no plans to change the exterior at all – to my mind it was perfect – and was concentrating at that time solely on the provision of those new bathrooms. The writing was firmly on the wall for that modern requirement, the en-suite bathroom. The neighbours wanted nothing done at all – a case of "not in my back yard" syndrome. In vain I repeatedly pointed out that doing nothing was not an option. Like so many others throughout the land, the old building had to modernise or die.

Eventually, with nothing left in my armoury to fend off their niggardly objections, I went to see the ringleader. A man almost three times my age, recently retired from a rich living in the City and the owner of a house that I would dearly have liked for my own, he sat me down and gave me chapter and verse, whilst rather looking down his be-whiskered nose at me. I was not offered the courtesy of a cup of tea or coffee and took that as an indication that the meeting was to be kept brief. It was clear that I was expected to cave in when he brought his big guns to bear in person, and to slink away to lick my wounds. I was an interloper to them, bent on ruffling the status quo, and I was therefore definitely not to be tolerated. He clearly had visions of fleets of lorries, and therefore noise, and the disruption of their quiet and sheltered life.

Noise? Noise from whom? A fleet of tipper-trucks and low-loaders? Carousing into the night by drunken country house revellers? I did my best to allay their combined fears, parrying with the fact that life must go on, that we were moving into more modern times. What would they prefer, my idea of an upmarket country hotel, or some other use that the building could be put to should I finally capitulate – and which might be infinitely worse for them? But no, he was not to be persuaded by any argument that I could bring to bear.

And I have a hatred since that day of being addressed as "my boy".

But I did take away one crucial thing from that meeting. He was only too aware of my failed planning applications because he had been one of the prime objectors, but he let slip the magic and heretofore unknown phrase "county specialist architect". I went back home and discovered that such a man really did exist and that he resided, probably in an ivory tower, in the county town some twenty miles away. It transpired that all planning applications for activity in conservation areas within the county passed over his desk before being referred back to the local council with his recommendation. Obvious, I suppose, once you know it.

He was thus the "go to" man that the planners deferred to in the cases that involved listed building or conservation areas, before they handed down their decisions to the likes of myself. I made an appointment and went to see him direct, cutting out the middleman, as it were. If he thought that that was a bit *avant-garde* on my part, he concealed it surprisingly well.

"Thank you for seeing me," I said with my best cheery smile, as I shook his hand.

"No problem, though I don't usually get members of the public coming to see me. Come and sit down."

We seemed to get on alright. Perhaps he was a little bit flattered that I had specifically sought him out to ask for his advice? After a lengthy chat in his office, explaining what I wanted to do, and showing him my plans, I invited him over for lunch to look over the place, reassuring him that it wasn't to be seen as a bribe. He was a wild-looking chap, in ancient corduroy trousers and a tweed jacket with leather elbow patches and the pockets stuffed full with who knows what, his unruly auburn hair flying all over the place and arms wind-milling about likewise as he and I walked through my list of proposals. The result? All I had to agree were some minor modifications, face was saved on both sides, and I got my initial permissions.

Over the years, we repeated that routine when I needed other work doing, and I had no other problems over planning. So, the work could finally start on putting in the bathrooms. There was a builder living at the other end of the village, and I regularly saw either his lorry or his van going to and fro. His wife and mine were friends of sorts and they used to share the kindergarten school run. He was a huge man sporting an equally huge scruffy blond beard. He came to see me one day, and his prices seemed very reasonable, so I let him loose on a couple of bathroom conversions to start with.

In hindsight, it was a quick introduction to the fact that the cheapest quote will seldom deliver the best work, but the bathrooms got me going, even with some decidedly dodgy pipework, which years later had to be ripped out and upgraded. I had, by then, learned that guests want to feel their en-suite bathroom is brand spanking new, as if nobody before them had used it at all! So, we had to get rid of those little six-inch square coloured tiles which had (looking back on it all) a hideous floral type pattern in a garish hue on them. Much bigger tiles, almost always bright shiny white, and power showers became the norm. How guest expectations have changed over the years! Those new showers though, resulted in us running out of hot water just when it was needed the most. Such are the daily conundrums in the life of an unsuspecting and inexperienced hotelier.

It was soon my turn to roll up my sleeves and crack on with decoration once the heavy manual labour had been completed. I decided that I could save quite a lot of money by painting bedrooms and bathrooms instead of using the services of a professional tradesman. I actually got quite good at it, disappearing into one of the bedrooms for hours on end, sloshing on the magnolia (everyone used magnolia in those days, didn't they?) and doing my best not to paint over edges. Nobody had yet introduced me to the existence or usage of masking tape, so that I could get a perfect straight edge by pulling the tape off afterwards. Once I learned that…well, I was away.

I must have painted every single one of those bedrooms myself over the first few years of my tenure. It had been a mammoth job, but gradually, as the years went by, I found that I had less time or inclination for painting and decorating, and so I started to use a local expert. I was so lucky to meet Reg, who lived in the same village and could walk to work when coming to me, though he seldom did. His van, or latterly his estate car, would draw up outside the front door and be abandoned there until I gently persuaded him to put it out of sight.

He became quite a regular fixture at the hotel because we needed to keep the place in tip-top condition, and that meant regularly covering with a new coat of paint almost everything that stood still. It is quite amazing how much superficial damage a regular throughput of guests will cause. They knock corners off corridor walls with their suitcases. They make marks on their bedroom walls, scuffing heaven only knows what along them. Chips appear in furniture as if by magic and light fittings are broken with monotonous regularity. They put down glasses on old tables and leave water marks behind. Suitcases are heaved on to beds instead of the luggage rack provided, leading to complaints of dirty bedspreads. Children seem to delight in scratching anything that they can lay their hands on as though they are required to carve their initials for future generations to wonder over. We soon learned not to leave any non-antique table bare, but to coat the surface in marine varnish, to give it a good finish whilst providing the required protection. I was so pleased that we had Reg to sort things out, though I would spend far too long chatting with him and picking up on the local gossip instead of attending to my business. But stuff such as that keeps one grounded and he was a bloke, surrounded as I was by a sea of women.

Another bloke who became a regular with us was Nigel. Dear Nigel took on the long-term maintenance of our garden. He mowed the grass, looked after the vegetable patch, tended the flower beds and hedges, and did sundry odd jobs. I was extremely fond of Nigel, who was short, stout of build and spoke with a very rural accent. I have no idea now where he originally popped up from, but one day, there he was, and he must have stayed for about fifteen years. Later, as he slowed up, I bought him a small ride-on motor mower. He loved that, whizzing up and down, doffing his flat cap to all and sundry.

When we first started properly on the rebuilding of the business, after the fire and the departure of the fearsome Miss Brown, I could not cook, other than the rudimentary offerings that a young bachelor prepares for himself when living in digs. But I was perforce a quick learner. My new livelihood was to depend on it. There was someone part-time that came in, and I filled in where necessary. It must have been pretty dire, but then on the other hand there weren't many guests to have to bother about. Guest expectation was not too high then, and we only offered a three-course set menu, so it was moderately easy to budget. There were no casual walk-in diners for us yet, and everybody who had pre-booked to stay overnight would invariably eat in, since there was nowhere else to go, and the offerings by the local pub were pretty grim.

I packed myself off to the local catering college to learn the basics, and put my newfound skills into practice in the evenings, should we be lucky to have guests. I spent afternoons up to my elbows in flour as I tried and failed to master the complexities of differing types of pastry. I fell in love with suet puddings, to the great detriment of my waistline.

I became the master of all sorts of soups reconstituted from large catering tins, garnished with some floating parley to offer a semblance of their being home-made. Then there was easy stuff like braised lamb chops with carrots and onions, stuffed hearts (remember, it was the '60s!) and liver and bacon with a rich onion gravy. All could be put on flat trays and just stuffed into the oven, almost impossible to ruin. I was pretty efficient at cooking roast chickens and the like, too. It was the golden era of the prawn cocktail at one end of the menu, and the black forest gateau at the other end. Everyone's favourites, those were, as well as a peach melba. Some frozen prawns with a sauce made of mayonnaise (previously salad cream) and tomato ketchup and a squeeze of lemon was a doddle; when I was feeling devilish, I might even sprinkle a dusting of paprika in to it, to give it a bit of a kick. Even easier was black forest gateau, because we bought it in, deep frozen, from a wholesaler and slathered fake whipped "whizzer" cream over it. A peach melba was, in those times, half a tinned peach sitting on a scoop of vanilla ice cream (also bought in) with a squirt of raspberry or strawberry sauce (whichever was to hand) over the top. We could not sell enough of that stuff. Oh, happy days, indeed they were!

Those tinned peaches also found their way into fruit crumbles. Apple crumble was always the favourite, but, oddly enough, tinned sliced peach crumble ran it a close second, and both appeared weekly on the menu, whatever the season.

I became a dab hand at making curries. Not perhaps ones that an aficionado might enjoy, but ones that suited the palates of the less genteel of our guests. Starting off with lobbing a couple of spoonsful of Madras paste into a kind of stew, I upped my game by obtaining some spices that I learned about from a cookbook and heated them in a pan to release the taste and aromas. My chicken curry went down a storm.

Sunday was decreed as the day off for our chef, and guess who had to stand in? Breakfast was a shoe-in, as they say over the pond. No problems for me with the likes of poached eggs; I have never understood the rigmarole that even some top chefs go through with whirling water and liberal doses of vinegar. I have always sent poached eggs back when I am staying at another hotel if they have been poached with vinegar; the taste is disgusting. Proper Manx kippers were also a favourite order. Sunday lunch was always a roast of some kind, and that was fairly straightforward. For dinner, I always settled on a salmagundi. I suppose that it is an old-fashioned dish, but it gave me the option of raiding through the fridges and using up all different types of leftover, to add to the nice cuts of meat that I displayed. It made a very colourful buffet and was much remarked upon by guests. From my point of view, it proved to be very economical, which was the main thing. But oh, how I used to hate the evenings when I had to cook in those early days. I was completely drained by the end of it, having been on my feet for fourteen hours or more.

I hated having to lever myself out of bed early on a Sunday morning, and hated, too, having to get up on Monday with my body still aching.

But, onwards and upwards, as the saying goes.

Chapter 3

New Arrivals

An unusual but very nice couple arrived one spring afternoon. They came to us quite out of the blue, pulling up outside and walking in through the door.

"Good afternoon. We're looking for a place to stay for quite a while, probably the whole summer. Is that something that might interest you?"

I liked them immediately.

I liked them even more when they asked about staying for about six months! He was a charming man, although it had to be said that he bore a more than passing resemblance to a caricature of an East End spiv, sporting wavy brilliantined hair and a droopy moustache. Do you remember Arthur Daley in *Minder*? The archetypal second-hand car salesman, more than happy to sell you the front end of one car, to which the back end of another had recently been welded? He was the spitting image of old Arthur. His lady, larger than average, it has to be said, billowed in like a galleon under full sail; her lipstick a slash of garish red that did nothing to match her attire, seemingly applied without resorting to the use of a mirror and probably whilst circumnavigating one of our notorious local potholes. Their powder blue Ford Cortina, a relic of a bygone age and sporting Spanish number plates, sat out there in the sunshine, its engine idly ticking away as it cooled down after its run from who knows where.

"Well, I am sure that we are going to be able to look after you," I said, not believing my luck. "Let me see... Yes, I have one of our larger twin-bedded rooms that I can show to you, and I can make it available to you for as long as you wish. Did I hear you mention up to six months?"

Oh, I loved those people on sight!

"Well, old chap, it could be as long as that. Let's say a definite couple of months to be going on with, shall we?"

We went and looked at the room and they seemed to be impressed, particularly with the almost brand new en-suite facilities, only recently installed.

"Would this be on a half board basis, then?" I enquired.

"Oh, no, I think that we would need to have lunch as well."

Full board! All my Christmases had come at once.

"No problem," I smiled, "I'll go and fetch your suitcases." Thinking to myself...before you change your minds.

I gave them a day or two to settle in and then my inquisitive nature got the better of me, and an opportunity presented itself for a bit of investigation. They were both English, and clearly well educated, that was obvious. They eventually told me that they were not married (well, not to each other anyway) but had been together for many years. They lived somewhere in Spain, I forget quite where now. The summer heat over there was getting too much for them, and so they had decided to bail out and come back to England for six months until Spain began to cool down a bit. Did they speak Spanish? No, I don't think so, barely a word, but then there are an awful lot of people that live abroad who have never learned the language of their adopted country.

They kept themselves to themselves, and each day they would pile into that powder blue Cortina and trundle off to visit places locally, keeping a low profile and troubling nobody.

On one occasion, I was invited to go with them to a watercress farm that they had heard of in the next county. I could hardly refuse, so I told the chef that he had better get to boning up on dishes that used a lot of watercress, because I was determined to bring plenty back with me. You can get bored with chilled watercress soup. We returned many hours later with the boot of the car full of watercress that he and I had picked, she being a little too grand to stoop and pick.

I briefly wondered more than once if they might be on the run from someone or something? It would appear not, because, when their six months was up, they loaded everything back into the Cortina, and set off on the long journey back to Spain. I stood and waved them off enthusiastically and thought that that would be the last we heard from them, but, true to their word, five months later a letter arrived asking for the same room in a month's time, and for a similar period. A deposit cheque, drawn on an English bank, was enclosed.

This went on for a number of years until the gentleman dropped down dead whilst they were in Spain. The lady said that she would like to come back to our hotel, because they had been so happy there together, and she really did not want to live any longer in Spain all by herself, particularly so because of the language problem. And so, one day she appeared with a load of luggage and took up residence in one of our single rooms. I don't know what happened to the Cortina; it was probably dumped on the Costa del Sol.

She and my mother took to each other, and it became quite the norm for them to go out some afternoons, either to a nearby town, or much further, down to the coast, and take afternoon tea or do a bit of shopping. On rainy days they stayed in and tea was taken in my mother's private sitting room. I was not very happy about having someone who could be seen as a permanent resident in the hotel, but, in view of my mother's advancing years, the friendship between them outweighed the drawbacks, and I remained content with the arrangement.

It transpired that the lady was very well connected socially, with titled family – two children, I think – that never came to see her more than once a year, and then under some duress, it appeared to me. They would take her out somewhere for lunch, bring her straight back, and then quickly disappear, not be seen again for a twelvemonth, their duty done as far as they were concerned. How sad. I never found out the full story.

Such things often end badly, and so it was in her case. She suddenly fell ill with some malaise or other, and her family decided that she should go into a nursing home. They didn't want the bother of looking after her themselves, disrupting their own lives. One day they arrived and collected her, without saying a word to us. She never returned to the hotel, though all her belongings remained in her room for three months or so. Nobody bothered to get in touch with me. I called the contact number that I had been given for one of the children and eventually one or other of them turned up and removed her things. I politely suggested that they should make some sort of payment to cover the time that her room had been occupied by her belongings and was therefore unlettable. Grudgingly, and under pressure, the bare minimum was offered after much haggling on their part.

I decided to have one last go on behalf of the staff. The lady had never left a tip for anyone.

"Would you care to leave something by way of a gratuity for the staff that have looked after your mother for so many months?"

"No," came the rapid reply, and they left; never, fortunately, ever to be seen again. No, they were not nice people at all.

I went back into the office and put some notes into the staff box when nobody was around.

The repository for old kitchen equipment and things that we could not find a proper home for elsewhere – a sort of detached Glory Hole – was a run-down but picturesque old outbuilding down at the far end of the front garden. It butted right up to the road passing along the edge of the property. Sturdily built of stone with a tiled roof, it must have been there for a couple of hundred years or so. Around it crept an aged ivy whose tendrils were beginning to lift the tiles away in one corner. Overhanging it were the branches of an ancient fig tree, and perhaps the roots were creeping into the foundations, such as they were. I had been meaning to do something about that outhouse for a long while, but there were, to my mind, more important things to attend to. Then, one morning as I was opening the post, I heard a loud rumbling crash, soon to be followed by the urgent tooting of motor horns.

On the off-chance that it might be of some interest, I ambled out, traversing the driveway and looked out to the scene over which disaster was writ large. I was horrified! The old outhouse had decamped in its entirety into the road. How it had got there was a mystery and has remained so to this day. Massive blocks of stone lay scattered along the verge. A couple of irate villagers were sitting in their automobiles hooting for dear life – as though that was going to do them any good. We had to get a neighbouring tractor to lift the blocks, later that morning, and deposit them at the side of the road until they could be taken away permanently and the road re-opened. A couple of villagers were late for their lunch that day. As usual, as the newcomer, it was deemed to be all my fault.

The upside was that we had cleared out all the useless paraphernalia from that outbuilding at a stroke, once and for all. The downside was that it left nowhere for certain members of staff to hide for a crafty smoke.

My wife at that time drove to work every day in a nearby town. Her car was a Ford Fiesta which was one day parked out in the private lane, directly in front of one of my mother's windows. I was having my elevenses in her sitting room when there was a hell of a crash, and the blue Ford simply disappeared from sight.

What on earth had happened?

I rushed out to find a motor cyclist, a young lad, picking himself up and dusting himself down after he had crashed straight into the back of the Ford, pushing it forward by some eight feet! He must have hit it at a heck of a lick. We brought him in and sat him down to get over the shock and to administer a bit of first aid in respect of facial grazing and sore elbows. His face, pimpled by acne, had taken on some heightened ruddiness and blotches from contact with the abrasive tarmac. Having established his name, which he was not at all comfortable to reveal, I telephoned to his home and spoke with his mother, who soon turned up and was most apologetic.

Needless to say, he had no insurance cover, nor money to pay for the extensive damage that he had caused to the rear of the Ford which by then displayed a large V-shaped indentation in the hatchback rear. It turned out that he lived on the council estate at the far end of the village, and his parents declined to assist him financially by way of any recompense. The police were not interested in him (other than the lack of insurance) because the accident happened on a private and unadopted lane. So, muggins here was left well out of pocket, having to fund quite an extensive rear-end rebuild, after which the Ford was never quite the same again, so it was swapped for an MG Midget.

At times, as the local lads would clatter home along the lane to the council estate after a heavy Friday night in The Malt Shovel, the sole remaining village pub, one or more of them got it into their mind to play a mild but irritating trick on us. Along the frontage of the hotel was a line of four bay trees in large faux lead tubs. They might have been faux lead but they were extremely large and heavy, those tubs. Often, I would walk towards the hotel on a Saturday morning and find that the tub at the end of the line, the one nearest to the lane, had been extremely carefully tipped over and was lying on its side. No earth had been spilt and no damage was ever done. Great care must have been taken over the operation.

Had the local ale given someone the strength of two, I used to mull, because it took two of us to get that tub back on its feet, no worse for wear? I never discovered the culprits. It went on for a few months, and then presumably the lad or lads got bored and moved on to a different target elsewhere.

Chapter 4

Fire!

A huge problem was to rear its ugly head in the '70s, and that was the bringing in of the new fire regulations for commercial properties. Naturally, these applied to hotels as well as to other types of business premises. The brigade officer from the nearest big town made an appointment to come and see me, and was then despatched to do a survey and to explain what I would need to have done in order for the hotel to comply with the new safety rules.

I had no idea what would actually be required, other than having read the more lurid reports in the newspapers, which had already resulted in more than a few sleepless nights for me.

A nice chap he was, that fire officer, as I remember, but he was feeling his way through the myriad of new demands, much as I needed to do. We sat down together and I gave him a cup of tea. Once the pleasantries were over, we did a walk around together.

"Well, the first thing that I notice is that every bedroom door will have to have self-closing devices fitted."

At my questioning raised eyebrow, he went on further. "There will also have to be an anti-smoke channel cut around each bedroom door." He was pointing out some lovely old original mahogany doors with their original brass fittings.

"Do you realise how old these doors are, and that they form part of the heritage of the building?"

"Not negotiable, I'm afraid, sir. Rules is rules, as they say. The new law makes no allowances for the type of premises."

"OK. Well, let's leave that for now and move on."

And so, it went on – magnetic closers on corridor doors; here, there and everywhere fire extinguishers and smoke alarms. I could see *£££* signs piling up to create significant inroads into my non-existent profit margin. A quick mental calculation resulted in me knowing that I was already "in the red".

It was to get worse. Much worse.

We arrived back at the bottom of my beautiful old original staircase, which swept upwards, light and airy, to the first floor, a major part of the history and fabric of the building. He had clearly been keeping the worst back until last.

"You will be able to keep that staircase, sir, but it will have to be fireproofed to my satisfaction. Let's go and sit down and then I can roughly draw out for you what I have in mind."

I tottered into the lounge, praying that nobody else would be about to see me tearing my already thinning hair out.

With a flourish, once we were seated, out came a sketch pad, on which he started to draw. He popped back out a couple of times with his pad, gazing up at the staircase and sucking thoughtfully on the end of his pencil, before finally showing me the results of his artistic flair. The outcome was that the bottom of the entire staircase, as well as the top, where it met the first-floor landing, would have to be encased in fire-proof glass with a fire-proof frame to hold it in place. The doors to be fitted at the top and bottom would be on self-closers, and there would have to be break-glass alarm points at top and bottom also.

Encasing that grand old staircase in fire-proof glass would be awful visually, historically and price-wise.

"Alarm points? Where, exactly?"

"Ah, I was just going to mention that. You see, in a place like this, you are going to have to install an automatic fire alarm system with a central control panel, but don't worry, we can go through that on my next visit. I think that you have quite enough to think about for today."

I ushered him out and went in search of a strong cup of tea – or it might have been a very large gin. There was no point in trying to discuss this with my mother as she was becoming slightly infirm and even more uninterested in the running of the hotel. What the hell was I to do? I simply couldn't afford to implement all that.

I took a rare afternoon off and drove a long way down to the sea. I took my mother with me to give her a bit of a change and having parked her on a bench on the promenade, I started walking up and down, trying to clear my head of unnecessary clutter. At the end of an hour or so I believed that I had got nearly everything into some sort of logical order and had come up with a number of questions that needed to be asked. The main sticking point would obviously be the cost, and whether the work could be phased in over a period of time to give me some financial breathing space, coupled with what was going to happen to my lovely staircase. I really had to dig my heels in on that one, but I couldn't see a way around it.

I collected mother and took her for tea at a smart hotel on the seafront. We walked in and a "light bulb" moment occurred.

"Mother, just look at that staircase!" I pointed it out to her.

"Yes, dear, isn't it nice." She hadn't clicked on the potential importance of exactly what we were looking at.

"No, look. It's completely open plan."

"Mmm, yes dear, how nice."

I plonked her down in the lounge, ordered some tea, and then went in search of the hotel manager, praying that he or she would be on duty. The hotel was owned by Trust House Forte, a large hotel chain, as it then was, and judging from the prominent fire regulation notices, it must have been inspected already and passed the requirements.

After a word with the young receptionist, the manager came out from his office. Short and portly, he obviously enjoyed the food at his hotel. We shook hands and I introduced myself, asking, after some pleasantries, "Have you been subject to inspection by your local Fire Authority in respect of these new regulations?"

Indeed, yes, they had. As a THF hotel they had probably been in the forefront of it all; in fact, it wouldn't have surprised me if someone on their main board had been on some sort of advisory panel and consulted in advance of the regulations being published.

"Well, my question is quite simple," I said to him, explaining my potential problem with the period staircase.

He shrugged noncommittally. "It was all handled by Head Office, I'm afraid. We had little or no input at this end. Contractors just came in with a list of the work that needed to be done." I supposed that THF wielded a bigger stick than I ever could.

"OK, well thanks for your time. At least it gives me some comfort."

My mother and I finished our tea and wended our way homewards. But it had set me thinking, and over the next few days I made it my business to chat to other hoteliers, and I visited a few hotels in the area, discovering at least two grand establishments that had been visited by their local Fire Authority, but managed to retain important architectural features.

We did a simple mock-up of what blocking in my glorious staircase might look like, and everyone to whom I showed it agreed that it would ruin the visual impact. But what was I to do?

The following week the fire officer returned with his formal plans. We sat down, and he showed me an outline of the type of electronic fire alarm system that I would be required to install. There were to be break glass points at strategic areas; new fire extinguishers, too. New wiring would need to be installed and chased into walls in order for it to be hidden from sight.

I left the fire officer with a parting shot. In the nicest possible way, having pointed out other hotels with a similar problem, I told him that over my dead body would we be enclosing our staircase in a wooden framework enclosing fire-retardant glass! The ball was put squarely back into his court.

"I'll report your views on that back to my superiors, sir, but don't hold your breath. As I said before, rules is rules." And with that, he was gone.

At this stage, I thought that the costs for all of this could break me, but, putting a brave face on it, I started to get in some prices. Big national fire services companies were quick to tout for business in the wake of the new legislation and I asked one to come to see me. They were a big household name nationally, seemed to have the right experience and could do the job within the time framework required. They offered a few comments on the scheme proposed by the fire authority and agreed to send someone to meet them to discuss some options.

Options? What options? Nobody else had told me that there could be options!

As they said to me: "There are always options. You just have to find them."

The clincher for me, over and above other companies that came along, was that they also offered deferred payment terms.

When the alarm system had finally been installed by them some months later, I called the fire authority and asked them to meet me on site for the required demonstration. A different officer came along. The new system was approved, though the staircase issue was still on the back burner. But he indicated that he did not require two of the manual fire extinguishers that had been bolted to the wall according to the previous Fire Authority produced plan, nor two of the new break glass points, with the wiring so expensively chased in.

"What do you mean, you don't want them?" I said, aghast.

"Well, technically, none of them are necessary in terms of providing the required safety measures."

"But we have been to a lot of expense to put them in!"

"Up to you, sir. They can stay or go."

"Well, now it's all there, it may as well all stay there. How come there's a change of plan?"

And with the answer came the utterly astounding information that different fire officers had the leeway to interpret things differently on the ground. How ridiculous was that?

And so, with that answer under my belt, I decided that it was time to call in the heavy mob. I rang up the BHRCA (The British Hotels, Restaurants and Caterers Association), the trade body of which I was a member, and put my concerns to somebody there. After the usual platitudes had been proffered, I was told that, because all of the fire regulation business being so new, they had retained as a consultant some nationally known and highly regarded technical expert to act on behalf of the BHRCA.

After a little pressure, they agreed to my direct approach on a private basis, which was just as well because the fire authority was still indicating that they would take me to court over my refusal to block in my staircase. I offered my situation as a test case for the BHRCA.

"No," came the immediate response.

"But surely you are going to have quite a number of members who will be affected by this particular issue? Surely it must be in your interests as our trade body?"

"Sorry, but no."

Would they like to make some contribution to my costs, then? Sadly, "No", yet again came the reply. I did start to wonder what real benefits I might have from being a member.

They agreed that I could approach the technical expert directly. A nice chap he was, but devilish expensive. He lived at the other end of the country and would only travel first class on the train. We agreed what I thought to be an astronomical fee to cover his visit. What alternative did I have? I met him at my local station – the first time in over a year that I had needed to go there other than for my regular dawn run to collect meat off the milk train direct from Smithfield.

Indeed, of course there were options, said my expert adviser; there were usually different ways of skinning the proverbial cat while remaining within the defined parameters of fire safety legislation. He was able to show me a number of hotels with far more imposing staircases left un-ravaged by the demon frosted fire glass. He put together a report for me and offered to come back again to testify on my behalf in the forthcoming court case. A further astronomical fee was mooted, and grudgingly accepted.

Armed with the report, I went to the fire authority HQ. I smacked it on the table and they simply caved in. Just like that! In less than five minutes it was all over, provided that I would offer the *quid pro quo* of installing a further three smoke detectors. That was all there was to it. It was all so very wrong. But months of worry, pain and heartache were shed like a snake sloughing its skin, and I emerged into a sunny day with the broadest of smiles.

Chapter 5

To Park or not to Park

A taxi from the railway station turned up one morning and decanted two stout middle-aged ladies who had booked a twin room with us for a fortnight. Oh, how I loved those golden, olden days when people went on holiday for a fortnight! Summers were booked solid long ahead, and it kept costs down and therefore profits up. Anyway, the two ladies came to the desk, voluminous cloak-style coats billowing, and cloche hats firmly askew, and checked in. They looked like extras from an old black and white Agatha Christie play. But I could see no luggage.

Then the front door banged open and in came the local village taxi driver, purple in the face from his strenuous exertions of literally dragging the most enormous suitcase that I had ever seen into the hotel. He puffed and wheezed, red in the face, and it was all that he could do to touch his forelock in response to the meagre tip handed over by one of the ladies.

It was our policy to take luggage to bedrooms for our guests, and indeed to bring it back down again when they departed. After the shenanigans with the taxi driver, I approached the suitcase with no little trepidation. I put my hand through the handle and lifted. Or rather, I didn't lift. The case budged not one iota. The handle stretched, but the case did not move. I really couldn't shift it, and there was no way that I was going to allow any of the staff to injure themselves trying to do so. My chef wandered past and offered, and he was indeed a big and brawny chap, but I could see in my mind him having days off for a rupture or whatever.

"Ladies, we have a problem. None of us can lift that suitcase up our stairs to your bedroom."

"Well, don't you have a lift?"

I sorely doubted whether a small hotel-type passenger lift would have hoisted it up anyway.

"No, I regret that we do not. This is an old period building, and there is no room for one. There is a solution to this, however, although you may not much like it."

And so, with much sighing and grumbling, they started to unpack some of their belongings in the hall and we transported them upstairs, until the suitcase became of a manageable weight.

It was a crazy situation, which assuredly they should have considered when they packed their case at home in the first place?

"But we only have the one case!" they chorused.

⁂

More people were arriving by car by then, and fewer by train – seldom nowadays did I need to go to the local railway station to collect our guests. This meant that a further project to be tackled when funds allowed was our limited car parking. I had seen the reaction from the disgruntled neighbours concerning my internal planning applications. Now, some ten years into my tenure, it was time to do something outside, and I saw problems ahead.

I had discovered, from poring over the original title deeds, that in addition to the hotel I also owned the rights to exclusive usage of the ancient and long disused local fire station which abutted the lane, to be held in perpetuity in exchange for my uninterrupted payment of an annual peppercorn rent.

To be entirely truthful, it was just a rotting corrugated-iron edifice, painted originally in a sort of camouflage dark green, which, someone had told me, used to house the village fire engine or engines in the last war. It had probably been some sort of Home Guard effort for the community. Technically, although it was a rusty corrugated iron structure, it too had automatically become a listed building within the surrounding conservation area. As such, it enjoyed a high level of protection against development at one end of the scale or demolition at the other.

It had no front doors (had it ever had any?), and was big enough to hold two old fire trucks; or nowadays, four cars, two in front and two behind. So, it was really a double-sized double garage, though I was petrified when anyone elected to park their car under its leaking roof. When I dreamed,

I dreamed of the whole thing collapsing onto guests' cherished cars. A storm would leave me with a sleepless night. I was careful to make no charge for vehicles brave enough to park within, and I put up a sign saying that we accepted no responsibility, though I had grave doubts as to whether such a disclaimer had any validity.

My mother, bless her, had one fine day driven her Renault straight into one of the main supporting wooden uprights and knocked it well adrift of the vertical. Nothing much happened, other than a few creaks and groans from rusty metal and rotting timber, and so we reinstated the post, reinforced it, and thought no more about it until later, when the insurers told me that they would no longer cover any vehicle parked in it. I was amazed that they had not said it years before. So, before anyone could complain, we took photographs of it from every angle and then we got a friendly neighbour with his tractor to push it over one stormy night, leaving a heap of rusty tin and rubble to be cleared the next morning. I photographed it again in its new horizontal format. To my utter astonishment, nobody said a word, other than my mother who complained that she had nowhere to park her car. There was not a whimper from the junta along the lane, who believed that it had just fallen down in the bad weather.

Fortunately, the base of the building had been concreted in the war as hard-standing for those fire engines, and so when we had properly cleared everything away we revealed parking space enough for six cars – two extra on the ramp leading upwards to it. And boy, did it all look smarter overall when we put a new oak post and rail fence around it.

Enter the church! Or rather the local representative of the diocese. He came by appointment and it was soon very clear that he came with a heavyweight complaint. The grumbling junta of owners along the lane had once again got their heads together and come up with yet another method of sticking the knife into my burgeoning business. I learned that they had complained to the church that our guests were parking their cars overnight in the lane, and restricting their ease of access.

Well, yes, there were cars parked in the lane, but no, there was no restriction of access, which at that point was double width. The lane was technically owned by the church, which was why the local diocesan representative was involved, although all owners of land along it had rights of access, and that included ourselves. I issued a challenge for the old deeds (made well before the advent of the motor car, even in its most primitive form) to demonstrate that right of access did not, per se, give an extension to park one's cart, or by later extension, motor car.

"Just what do you want me to do about it?" I asked.

"Well, frankly, I really don't know," he said, scratching his head and easing a further chocolate digestive from the plate in front of him. "But we have to do something. They are all up in arms."

"Yes, that's all very well, but they have no counter proposal other than to try to ban my guests' cars from parking in the lane. That's just not going to happen, because it would be the end of things for me, just as we are starting to expand."

Yes, we were using up more of the lane-side parking, but it was not inconveniencing anyone. His argument roundly rebuffed, he went on his way, but I was careful to leave the door wide open for further parlay. It was soon to arrive, and from various quarters.

Firstly, came the leader of the junta. "We never complained about you knocking down the old fire station, did we?"

Well, no, they didn't, but what was it to do with them anyway? By doing so, I had created more off-lane parking. They should be applauding me. I fleetingly thought: so how did you know we demolished it accidentally-on-purpose?

Closely following them came the church representative and his sidekick once again. "We have discovered that parishioners are finding it more and more difficult to park their cars on Sundays for the services over the road."

"Really!" I said. "You mean parking in a private lane where they technically have no right to park motor cars at all, according to the diocese?"

"Ah, but the vicarage has acquired rights over the lane from old bye-laws!"

"Well, tell them to park in front of the vicarage then. Oh, and if that is so, then we must have acquired the same rights!"

He couldn't argue that point. We reached an impasse, and it was the moment for a glass of sherry to be proffered. I left them to stew for a couple of weeks before I offered them the perfect solution.

That solution lay in the field on the opposite side of the lane to the hotel. It was a very large field, almost in the centre of the village, and it had a tarmac path across it as a right of way from time immemorial. I offered to sign a long lease on that field which was owned by the diocese – it was glebe land. In addition, for a small annual payment, I would agree to maintain the field, mow it when necessary, and keep the fence boundaries in good repair. Bearing in mind that the field was some nine acres in size and contained some superb mature oak trees, it was quite a lot to take on, but I scented promotion and publicity.

In exchange for my commitment, I advised them that I wanted very little. Just enough church land to be made over to me – freehold, of course – for me to extend my existing car park, so ridding everybody permanently of the problem of car parking on the lane.

Have you ever tried to buy land from the church? There are hoops by the million to be jumped through just to get to first base – agreement in principle to sell. The church is not keen to sell any of its land.

Through layer after layer of bureaucracy we all had to wade before a glimmer of light shone, months before final agreement was reached. The ink was hardly dry on the conveyance before I had a JCB digger moving in the following week and a tarmac construction company then finished the job soon thereafter to lay out a brand-new car park with enough spaces marked out for all my foreseeable needs. An oak post and rail ranch fence was erected to keep at bay the cows that I had put onto the field, and everyone seemed happy. Me? I was ecstatic!

Little did I realise that on the following Sunday all the churchgoers would completely take it over. Instead of parking in the lane, they assumed that I had created a new car park just for them – despite the large new sign informing of privacy for hotel guests. Some turned quite unnecessarily aggressive about it all, and I was left with no alternative but to invoke a threat of clamping – a very new-fangled idea at that time.

That new car park was one of the best things that I had done at the hotel since taking over. It really looked impressive with the spaces lined out on the tarmac, the oak post and rail fencing and the newly planted hedging screen. I invited the local press around for the grand opening, and I got a great friend of mine who was a proper celebrity to open it. We had an inquisitive audience for the ceremony consisting of my cows, who leant over the new fence as though to get a closer look. When it was all over and the ceremonious glass or two of bubbly had been taken, I rushed back outside when the first guests drove up and parked on it, stupidly looking for smudges on the white lines, or whatever. As they got out of their car they must have thought that I was the local version of Basil Fawlty.

All was perfect thereafter for quite a while and there was a prolonged silence from the cohort of grumblers along the lane. But I really got a bit irate about certain churchgoers who would leave their cars on my new car park before attending morning and evening services.

They knew it was private parking for the sole use of hotel guests, but they simply ignored the fact, and otherwise had no intention of making use of the hotel even though it was in walking distance from the church. Worst of all was when they parked in good time for vespers, and then my new incoming guests could find no parking space on arrival. It led to a number of rows and culminated in me deciding that I was left with no other option than to go ahead and put up a polite notice to the effect that parking of cars for churchgoers on our car park would no longer be tolerated and that vehicles would be henceforth subject to the new-fangled and dreaded clamp, recently all the rage in the tabloids.

Although I was well aware that such clamps existed, I had actually no idea whether they could be bought privately, nor indeed whether they were legal in circumstances such as mine. It was all a bit of a bluff on my part.

One of our long-standing coffee shop clients was dear old Mrs Onions – she pronounced it O'Nyons – who came in for coffee the next day and sought me out, asking what she should do on Sunday morning now that my sign had gone up.

"Good morning. Sorry to trouble you, but I've seen that notice that you've put up. What is clamping?"

"Hello Mrs Onions, how nice to see you. A clamp is a large lump of metal that can be attached to one of your wheels in order to prevent the car being driven away."

"But why would anyone want to do that?"

"Well, the problem is that the new hotel car park – which actually cost me a lot of money – is being overrun by churchgoers and then there is nowhere for my guests to park. I'm sure that you understand? I really have to do something, and this is my last resort."

"So how much are you going to charge to release a clamped car?"

Well, that rather stumped me. In the end I went around and asked the vicar if he might say a few words to his next congregation. That worked a treat and I had fewer parking problems for a while.

A small film team came to stay one night. They had been commissioned to put together the sales brochure for the new Vauxhall Cavalier – that is to say the very first of the many iterations of the Cavalier, which shows how long ago it was – and their organisation had identified a particular stunning location for a dawn shoot to introduce the car dramatically to the general public.

My wife and I got talking with them in the bar that evening, and it transpired that they were lacking a key feature of the shoot, which was to take place very early the following morning. They had it all mapped out, down to the exact location which had been scouted out beforehand. Although they had brought the new car along with them, tantalisingly sheeted over on a trailer, they had forgotten about the need for occupants for the car.

My wife, being a rather decorative lady – she still worked as an in-store beauty consultant for Helena Rubinstein – fitted the bill perfectly as the passenger, and, not to be left out from this jaunt, I was chosen to be the driver.

And so, at some quite ungodly hour, we all assembled outside the hotel and moved off in convoy to the selected site, some half an hour away, ready to be filmed. In position as dawn broke, we saw the first shafts of watery yellow sunlight appear over the horizon to burn away the morning mist which began to clear, leaving the Cavalier and ourselves bathed in golden light on a track beside a field of ripened waving corn, with the turrets of a distant castle poking through the horizon mist. And so, it was that we appeared in the final take for that commercial for the new car, although it was all filmed from my wife's side of the car and I was in shadow. If I remember correctly, we were offered £60 cash as our fee, which I hurriedly pocketed. They even sent me a copy of the final Vauxhall brochure, with ourselves on the cover. Sixty pounds was good money in those days, and it well compensated for getting up at about 4 a.m.

Talking of cars, we had a booking come in from Japan for a few nights one summer. At the appointed time, a deep rumbling bark could be heard on the driveway, which then died away instantly, as racing engines do when shut down. A few minutes passed and then a couple of Japanese gentlemen came to the desk, rather incongruously decked out in tweeds. They politely checked in and were shown to their rooms, asking if their car would be all right left where it was. I was interested in the very special noise that had come from the car that they had arrived in and then just abandoned; so, after they had gone upstairs I walked outside, just idly to check it out, and there was a dark blue racing Jaguar D-type, with a world-famous white band across the front of the bonnet. A real original, not a kit car – it was probably worth well north of a million pounds even in those days. I had to pinch myself as I blinked at it in awe.

I tottered back in and rang up to their rooms. "I am so sorry to trouble you, but could one of you pop downstairs please when it is convenient?"

A few moments later they both arrived at the desk, smiling and bowing. I was almost lost for words, and, after gulping a couple of times…

"It really is real, isn't it?" I enquired, still pinching myself, getting more worried by the moment. I was a bit tongue-tied.

"Oh, yes indeed, it really is! We have come over to England from Japan on a motoring holiday, and we are booked in to take it to a couple of events while we are here, and next week we are going down to the Loire valley in France with it for a big meeting."

I was struggling a bit with reality here. Would my insurers cover it should there be an accident in the night? What would be my liability if it was stolen? What on earth was I to do? They, for their part, seemed completely relaxed. Perhaps it was a cultural thing? Or perhaps a million quid was just pocket money to them?

All I could think of was to back my own car out of the garage at my cottage and put the D-type in there. And so, we did just that, and they were so grateful to me that they wrote a couple of weeks later, enclosing photographs of their car at some stupendous event in the Loire valley. There must have been at least a dozen C- and D-types parked in a line outside the front of a lovely chateau. I still have those pictures. It had been just the most amazing surreal encounter!

Chapter 6

Busman's Holiday

Carol decided that I needed a holiday. Who was I to argue? She was my right hand.

I was never very good at taking holidays, and it must have been a number of years after I first came to the hotel that I finally managed to find both the time and the money to take one. During all that time, I was under a lot of strain. Not only was I having to try to juggle the needs of my wife and son in trying to have a modicum of home life, but the seemingly never-ending requirements of the hotel were resulting in me having to be on site for very lengthy hours. If I was not cooking, I could be found painting a bedroom, filling in for any member of staff that had called in sick (or just not turned up) or trying to find a non-existent quiet corner where I could draw breath and seek to get my mind around just what to do next, whether that be a day forward, or more strategically months ahead when I might have accumulated a bit of money into the hotel coffers to be spent on urgent improvements, like fixing the roof.

At times like those I could readily understand that initial reluctance of mine to take on what seemed then to be a crazy proposition.

My mother continued to be a tower of strength to me. Sitting with her over a cup of tea, I could use her as a sounding board, although it was very much a one-way street, as she displayed virtually no interest in the future development of things as mundane as lavatories or bedrooms. She waved most of it aside, more interested in finding out when I would next take her to the races. Since my wife was still working as a beauty consultant behind a counter of a big store, it was difficult to bring her on board, as by the time that I left the hotel I was more than ready to get some sleep.

However, and who can blame them, it seemed to be of vital importance to every single member of staff to prioritise their need for their annual holiday, so much so that there had to be a holiday rota board created in order to avoid key people being off at the same time. Each year there was a scramble for people to get their names on that board and there was much competition to jostle themselves into position ahead of their peers and grab whatever they deemed to be the prime spot first. Of course, as we moved onwards through the early part of the year, they would then try to change their dates as the wishes of their family and friends intervened.

But that year I beat them all to it. When I created the holiday board, I blanked out two weeks in the summer for us to go away. We had made an early booking to go to Tunisia. There was absolute uproar in the ranks! How could I – merely the owner of the hotel – seek to take precedence over the rest of them? I explained that it was a done deal and they should get over it.

The date finally came around. We said our goodbyes and a rickety old aeroplane (was it really a Dakota?) lifted off from the runway to take us to the sparkling blue waters and golden sands of the coastal area of Tunisia. The hotel was all that we could have expected, and it was simply a world away. I found the week on the beach in a hot climate, doing absolutely nothing for most of the day, was not only a refreshing change but therapeutic too, enabling me not only to recharge my batteries, but to ponder the way forward without interruption. After that week it was back to the familiar grindstone, and Tunisia quickly became a fuzzy blur in the memory, but I would return to the fray with a calmer brain and keener eye. A hotelier is never totally off duty, though, and every hotel that I went to or stayed at was subjected to intense scrutiny in every area into which I could poke my nose. I amassed, over the years, a wealth of knowledge and benefits that I was able to apply to my own business.

When I was a child, we had stayed in hotels as a family, of course. One of the nicest, I remember, was the Golf Links Hotel near Castletown on the Isle of Man. We went there on a number of occasions, probably so that my father could get in a game of golf each day, but possibly also because he had been briefly stationed on the island during World War Two, when he went through that OCTU course for officers, based in Douglas, the island capital. The hotel ran just perfectly, it seemed to me as an early teenager, a model of all that an hotel should be. Everything was in its place and ran so very smoothly, though in a gloriously old-fashioned way. I had been allocated a small single bedroom quite near to that of my parents, but I clearly remember that, though small, it was furnished so as to give an impression of space. The double-glazed window looked out over the tennis court to the rear of the hotel together with a wonderful view of the rocky shore and sea beyond. My parents, on the other side of the main corridor, could look out over the curved sweep of Derbyhaven bay and across to the tiny airport at Ronaldsway where a bi-plane was parked on the apron. I would sit in the old dark panelled bar before dinner with my parents whilst they consumed their drinks, before being shown into the dining room. We went back year after year and I loved the place. I recall that, in terms of expectation, it seemed to exceed in all departments. So, even then, it would appear that I was taking subliminal notice.

One year, my wife and I managed a holiday to the Italian Lakes, driving down there uneventfully apart from our overnight stop at the Hotel de la Côte d'Or at Saulieu where the chef proprietor enjoyed a coveted Michelin star, though we were unaware of that fact when I booked. It might even have been two stars, but I forget now. Desperately pompous service was the order of the day in the restaurant, and I remember little of what we ate. My sole memory of the place was that, having chosen my main course, I was asked by the head waiter for my choice of vegetable as accompaniment. I asked for green beans, only to be informed that they would not serve green beans with that dish as it was "inappropriate". Many years later, I learned that the chef-patron had committed suicide. It was said that he was depressed at the thought of losing his second Michelin star.

Arriving at our destination in Italy, we stayed right on the edge of Lake Como at the Grand Hotel Tremezzo, a gracious old lady sat in manicured grounds and with a frontage, just over the road, to the lake and to a pontoon for summer swimming, together with the required moorings for those famous Riva speedboats owned by the local glitterati. Each day we would motor to one lake or another, enjoying my Fiat 124 coupé which behaved faultlessly throughout the trip. Nowadays, that hotel is firmly in the unaffordable bracket as far as I am concerned. One George Clooney lives just up the road – and I can see why! These trips were precious times because of the need to get away from the business, allowing me to recharge my batteries. Nice hotels were also a breeding ground for new ideas to bring back and to put into practice as and when I could afford them.

When we first went to Tenerife, a beautiful island to which I would eventually make plans to retire, but that was far into the future, we travelled on Freddie Laker's Skytrain. It was a huge aeroplane for those days, and we thought it to be impossibly glamorous, though nowadays it would most likely be known colloquially as "cattle class".

We booked into a smart looking hotel called the Hotel Gran Tinerfe, in a small seaside village in the south of the island, half an hour or so from the southern airport. That little village was called Playa De Las Americas, and it would hit the headlines a couple of years later big time when somebody spread the rumour that actress Elizabeth Taylor and her friend Richard Burton were going there/had stayed there/were building a holiday home there. Probably none of those was actually true, but it spurred a frenzy of buyers trying to cash in on the next holiday hot spot.

We did not go back for a number of years, taking our young son Marcus, by then a toddler, for his first experience of life abroad. How it had all changed.

By then, Playa De Las Americas was on its way to becoming a vast concrete jungle with holiday homes creeping up the hillsides and more hotels than you would think possible in such close proximity to one another. It was the time of a boom in the package holiday trade, and Spain was right at the forefront of new ideas to please their rapidly expanding resorts and clientele.

We stayed in a brand-new hotel on the beach on a package holiday where the tour operator had skilfully managed to blank out from their brochure photographs the building site next door, where cranes, diggers and cement mixers all got together to make life a bit of a misery. A cacophony of sound would rouse us from our slumbers at the crack of dawn each day, covering us in dust and giving us headaches. Spanish workmen start their day early to avoid the heat of the sun later on. They are also addicted to their portable radios which all seemed to play different music at full decibel levels.

The only plus side was that we were among the first to get breakfast and lay out our towels on the nearby beach, so getting one up on the German contingent.

I had first visited to St Tropez on a camping holiday to the south of France with two other school friends when I was eighteen. We took my newish (but old original type) Mini Traveller which was painted in a garish shade of pale blue. It was a bit cramped in that little car, what with all the camping gear. I had never camped before, and, in my innocence, was quite looking forward to the experience – and what an experience it was going to be. The things that I remember most were the lines of ants that trekked over us and our sleeping bags each night, the nudist beach at Pampelonne (no, not for us), and the hordes of apparently very rich people that walked up and down the quayside, strutting their stuff for all the local barflies to see.

We three intrepid ex-schoolboys soon moved on to other less expensive places. We fetched up in Menton, a lovely town further along the coast, but fell foul of the weather when our tent was literally washed away on our second night as a result of a sudden and tremendous thunderstorm. The campsite was situated on a slight incline, and we found ourselves further down the slope than we were when we went to bed. But who thinks of things like that?

We packed up what we could, abandoning some gear and clothing that we could no longer find. We headed inland towards the Alps, but it was so cold when we parked again that we had the engine running most of the night with the bonnet of the car sticking into the flap of the tent. I wonder that we weren't gassed. Giving up once again, we broke down on the road back to Paris, at an appropriately named village that translated as World's End. A kind Frenchman offered to give us a tow to the next village. He set off as though the bats out of hell were after him and I had no option but to hang on for dear life, as I couldn't hoot at him because the battery was flat. If he happened to glance in his rear-view mirror, which I doubted, he probably thought that our wild gesticulations were an encouragement to proceed more rapidly. Half a day later, and after minor repairs, we continued at a more sedate pace to Paris. The final ignominy of that holiday was to be locked out of our Parisian campsite because we came back too late at night. The car had to stay at the side of the road, and we had to scale a wall to get back inside. Never were the white cliffs of Dover a more welcoming sight.

On my second visit to St. Tropez, many years later, my wife and I clattered into town in my MGB after an uneventful journey down the old N7. We were accompanied by friends who had never driven abroad, running in convoy with us in their powder-blue Jaguar E-Type, and petrified of getting separated from us. On arrival in the town, at a pre-arranged café, we met a very attractive, bronzed, blonde holiday representative named Clare, who showed us to our accommodation on the first floor of a hideous modern apartment block on the outskirts of town. There was no air conditioning, and it was furnished more akin to a hostel. No matter, though, as we would only need the place to lay our heads, and we were young then.

Clare turned out to be a bit of a character, spending her summers in St Tropez or similar upmarket resorts before wending her weary way home to mummy and daddy who owned a pile in the Home Counties. No doubt daddy was "something in the city". There she would have a breather to recuperate before jetting off to the ski slopes, taking on her *alter ego* as a chalet girl in Verbier. Such a hard life she made it out to be!

Our friends with the E Type, who had more money than we, were billeted in a small hotel right on the port, complete with a sea view. Very soon we re-discovered all the magic of the place and could understand just why it was a magnet for the moneyed glitterati. We all enjoyed an excellent holiday together, visiting old haunts and finding new ones.

The slightly more glamourous half of the duo in the E-Type sported a blonde wig. She always had that wig on. You could, as they say, see the join. No matter, she was very decorative for all that – and well she knew it. We were only ever to see her wig-less on one occasion during our long friendship, and that was when we went to the long sandy beach outside St Tropez for the first time. After settling herself on the pristine golden sands, having had her husband rush about to secure sunbeds and parasols, she divested herself of the wig, and carefully arranged it on a small plastic stand out of the direct sunlight.

My jaw dropped open, not just because of the wig stand, but because she appeared, on inspection – not too close, you understand – to have lovely, fine golden hair, which would have been a crowning delight for most ladies. All very strange. I could only think that it was something to do with the fact that her husband owned a chain of hair salons, and that she was his muse.

Many years later, I was once again to visit St Tropez. The father of my best man owned a superb sixty-foot motor cruiser that he maintained, with a crew, at Port Vauban by Antibes and I was invited for a couple of weeks on board. I got my sea legs on the short cruise from Antibes, arrived in the port area of St Tropez and docked on the end of one of the quays, where the prime requirement seemed to be to take on board huge blocks of ice to keep us going for the next two weeks. The holiday was abruptly cut short due to seriously bad weather in Corsica and we suffered the ignominy of having to take the big ferry back to Nice in order to collect the car. Yet another not very successful holiday!

I have read in the newspapers that there is a general statistic that states that everyone should expect to be burgled at least once in their lifetime.

My wife and I had been away on to mainland Spain, and the final days had descended into the grand-daddy of domestic dramas. Partly as a result, we ended up on a plane from Malaga earlier than we had originally expected. Exhausted (well, certainly on my part), we arrived back at my cottage across the lane from the hotel. I shall always remember the strange feeling of being unable to process exactly what was going on as I stood in front of the door and put the key in to the lock. I had a premonition of something being wrong, but I couldn't put my finger on it.

I went in through the porch and stopped dead. I saw a DVD recorder sitting on an armchair. I knew that had to be wrong, but, at a time such as that, the brain does not compute properly. I blinked and looked around, noticing that there were wet, dark brown and muddy footprints on the lounge carpet. Yes, wet, and therefore very recent! Stranger and stranger, I thought, until the obvious kicked in.

"Bloody hell, we've come back right in the middle of a burglary!"

"Well," said my wife, "for heaven's sake don't go inside any further. They might still be in there!"

But you just do, don't you? Outrage and the red mist took over.

And with that, throwing caution to the winds, I grabbed a walking stick from the stand just inside the front porch, and, with what I hoped was a blood-curdling shriek, galloped through into the rest of the house. In retrospect, it was probably a daft thing to do.

There were dark brown muddy footprints everywhere; in the lounge, the dining room, kitchen and tracking up and down the staircase. Piles of belongings were neatly placed ready near to the shattered back door, which was hanging loose on its hinges, preparatory to the attempted haul presumably being spirited away over the back lawn, across the field, and ending up who knew where.

The villains? It didn't take long to establish that they were not on the premises, but it must have been a very close shave. They must literally have light-footed it out the back as we unlocked the front door.

I had a small collection of Royal Crown Derby china, about 30 pieces in all. I used to buy a plate or cup from time to time when I saw that particular pattern available in the sales. All of it was gone, except, bizarrely, for a solitary egg cup residing on a lonely cupboard shelf in the dining room.

My wife had the presence of mind to pick up the telephone and called the police. There was still a small police station in our village, and in due course the local bobby turned up on his trusty bicycle. He had a look around and called in to his superiors. What did they do about it? Did they find the culprits? No, they made no progress at all, stating that my possessions would by then have been "fenced" within the local underworld, and what could they do?

What local underworld? What could the police do? I was outraged! What were they there for?

I mulled over, for a long time, just how it came about and that, apart from some electrical goods which were easily replaceable, the main haul had been all of that Crown Derby and some silver. Who knew about that? Had we taken a later plane as planned, it would all have been over and done with before we got back. I still ponder the thought of it having been an "inside job".

I had a very stout back door fitted to replace the old one, complete with locks and hinges more suited to the keep in a castle. Better late than never, I thought.

Chapter 7

The Forgotten Negligée

A very nice couple spent a long weekend with us. They were both middle aged, and she was very well preserved, statuesque and extremely attractive, with her blonde hair immaculate in a stylish chignon. It would take a person of stronger willpower than I not to notice her shapely legs, which seemed to go on for ever. They clearly enjoyed their room with a genuine antique four-poster bed, because they spent a lot of time in it – the room I mean, though perhaps also the bed. All very touchy-feely, if you know what I mean.

They seemed to be having a lovely break, whizzing off in his long-bonneted Morgan sports car down to the coast one day, and taking a picnic up into the hills on another. In the evenings, for their dinner by candlelight, our more expensive wines would be ordered, the most expensive items on the menu would be chosen, and loving glances would be exchanged between them, as though they had the entire room to themselves. Oh, that my wife looked at me like that!

After they had checked out, as late as possible, with me having wished them well, and with the hope that we would see them back again soon, I thought no more about them until the chambermaid presented me with a rather fetching silken negligée later that morning.

"I found this 'ere flimsy hanging on the hook on the back of the bathroom door, sir."

"Oh dear, which room was that?"

"The one that them nice couple had, as went a while back today."

I suppose that I was still a bit green. I parcelled up the item and posted it off to the address left in the visitors' book on the table in the hall, with a nice little personalised note to the effect that I hoped that they had enjoyed their stay, and that we might see them back at the hotel before too long.

A couple of days later, and the telephone rang. A very well-spoken lady was on the other end, icily calm, enunciating each word with that perfect diction and cut-glass accent which used to be known in the good old days as BBC English.

"Might I be speaking with the manager?"

"Well, madam, I am the owner of this hotel. May I help you?"

"In that case, I am ringing to thank you for sending me that silk negligée back."

"Madam, it was a pleasure!" But for some reason I was beginning to feel a bit queasy; the voice was not as I remembered, and alarm bells were starting to ring. "I do hope that you enjoyed your visit?"

"Well, my husband obviously did, but unfortunately it was not I that was with him."

The penny quickly dropped. I later received a letter from her solicitor asking me to confirm that the aforesaid negligée had been found in my hotel on that specific date. I supposed that a divorce would soon be in the offing.

From that day onward, we kept a box under the stairs into which all items left in the hotel were stored and tagged as to when and where they had been found. We kept items for 6 months and then disposed of them. Staff were never to return anything to anyone unless they specifically received instructions to do so and after the item had been properly identified.

That had been a hard-earned and uncomfortable lesson.

Unacceptable behaviour in a country house hotel came in many formats, often through an excess of libation or testosterone, including people exchanging bedrooms in the middle of the night. What couples got up to in the privacy of their rooms was their own affair. It was not up to me to interfere unless their actions were illegal or impacted on other guests or my staff. I was not there to police the morals or ethics of my guests.

Creaking floorboards, so beloved by the film industry for a particular genre of film, are a fact of life in an old country house, and they contributed occasionally to the hilarity.

Wife swapping, as it was called back in those heady days of the 70s, was an activity that seemed to go hand in hand with a country house hotel. I suppose it was the perfect venue: sufficiently impersonal, and with good food and plenty of beverages on hand to relax and fuel the libido towards a crescendo of excitement.

Such parties always fell into one or another camp. The former – and more tolerable to me – was where two couples would come for dinner and stay the night. The ritual of the keys was unnecessary, and they would just go about their nocturnal business discreetly with no harm done and no inconvenience to other guests. Coy looks over breakfast were often the most obvious giveaway, and the first we would know of it, if indeed we ever did know.

On the other hand, when throwing car keys (yes, they really did do that!) into an ash tray after dinner and brandies was done in full view of other guests, amidst much ribald or coarse comment, I took a dim view and was not averse to making my point of view known. Discretion should be the watchword. It was something that we frowned upon seriously, despite the fact that it brought in much needed extra revenue.

A typical scenario might go as follows. Four or five couples would make a reservation as a group, much as when going for a racing or golf weekend. But in this case, dinner would descend into louche comments and much sexual innuendo. Whether it was car keys or a number of alternatives, people would pair off and disappear upstairs, sometimes leaving just one couple staring uncomfortably at each other. These were the ones who had drawn the short straw and not found an exciting new partner for the night, being left behind to sort it all out as best they could. In a couple of cases, it was literally a husband and his own wife who had been so unfortunate as not to have been paired off with others.

Glossing over the activity through the night, breakfast time always presented a sorry group of males and females, looking much the worse for wear, and also looking decidedly uncomfortable in front of their spouses for having presumably over-enjoyed their illicit overnight trysts. The glossy ladies of the night before were long gone – hair styles all askew, and with bags under their eyes – leaving us to ponder why…

When any of the couples were local and known to us, they received an immediate – privately whispered – ban from further visits, issued when their account was presented for payment.

I was invited, on one occasion, to make up the numbers along with my wife. The answer was a firm "no" and I surely must have forgotten to mention it to her.

I also disapproved of individual male guests suggesting that a pretty village waitress might like to accompany them upstairs later in the evening. That was quite a regular occurrence, because staff were encouraged to present themselves smartly in their uniforms as befitted an upmarket hotel. Lone businessmen seemed to think it was their prerogative and that they were doing the girl in question a favour. When one chap, shouting the odds after dinner in the bar, told me to mind my own business, he too had to leave immediately, in a hurry.

"Perhaps you could come to the desk. I am making up your account."

"But, but, you can't do that! Where will I go at this time of night?" He was quite astounded.

"That's up to you, sir."

"I'm going to report you to the authorities for this!" He exploded, spittle flying.

"Do feel free, sir. Which particular authority do you have in mind? May I help with any phone numbers? I'm sure that they will all be interested in exactly why you are leaving."

He had brought this problem firmly upon himself, I decided.

I was just locking up one night when an internal call came through to me.

"This really is too much," spoke an irate guest, in answer to my query as to how I might be of assistance. "We have been trying to get to sleep for some time, but there is this banging noise, seemingly from the next room, as though a pipe is knocking away with an airlock in it. What can you do?"

Well, that was a new one on me. What indeed could I do? Why should a pipe be rattling with an airlock at that time of night? When I checked, the room next door to my complainant was let, so there was only one thing for it. I had better go and see what had gone wrong. Perhaps if I ran the basin taps for a bit…

Up the ancient staircase and along the corridor I walked, trying not to make a noise as I trod on old protesting floorboards, their creaks masked by the carpet runners. I paused and listened outside the bedroom door, and sure enough, I could hear a rhythmical tapping noise.

I knocked, but there was no response. The noise continued. I knocked again, this time more loudly and authoritatively. The knocking noise stopped instantly!

A minute later, and a tousled head popped round the door. "Yes?"

"May I come in?" I asked, and, as I saw the head retreat, I pushed the door open slightly and peered into the room. And there I saw the reason for that knocking noise.

A buxom lady, past the first flush of youth, it had to be said, was kneeling on the bed, stark naked, and it appeared that her hands were tied to the brass bedposts at the head of the bed. She blushed a deeper shade of red than from her recent exertions, and attempted, unsuccessfully, to cover her modesty, something that was entirely impossible due to her silken bonds.

I stood transfixed at the Rubenesque sight before me. I tried to look away, but my mind could not assess what my eyes were seeing, and my head would not turn. However, it was time for me to make a strategic retreat, save only to pass the comment that I hoped that they would enjoy the rest of their evening, but in so doing, to kindly do their best to stop the brass bedposts from knocking on the wall.

I tottered off downstairs, completed the regime of locking up, and went to bed. I slept uneasily, not being able to get certain images out of my mind.

I saw the couple the next morning after breakfast. They were at the front desk collecting a packed picnic lunch; he mild mannered and totally nondescript, unkempt and slender; she tall, and wearing an immaculately tailored suit.

Both smiled to me, and bade me a good day, a wish that I heartily reciprocated. No more was said, nor needed to be said.

A gentleman and a lady arrived one mid-morning, headed into the lounge and ordered coffee. They had decamped from a top-of-the-range maroon Jaguar coupé and walked in holding hands. Half an hour into their visit, the man popped out of the lounge, leaned over the reception desk, and said:

"This looks a lovely hotel. We would like to stay please, if you have a double room?"

"Certainly sir, may I take some details please?"

He signed the visitors' book, and said: "How much will it be, please? I may as well settle up now. It's just for the one night, you know." And with that he handed over a wad of cash. "No need for a bill, you know."

They were shown up to their room, one of our quirkier ones with a slightly sloping floor, so that the large double bed was jacked up a couple of inches at the front end in order for it to be absolutely horizontal. There were other nice period features in the room, which still had fitted, in a cupboard, one of those old electric slot meters that used to be in fashion so many years ago, for the guest to pay for their own electricity – that just tells you how this place had been occupied and how mean the owner!

Three hours or so later, he appeared back at reception, saying: "I've just had a phone call, and I am needed back at the office, so we shall have to go. So sorry… Lovely here… 'Bye."

I thanked him for returning his key and commiserated with him. I thought it a bit strange because it was before we had installed telephones into bedrooms, and mobile phones were still the size of bricks and quite rare. I soon forgot about it.

Blow me down, the same maroon Jaguar turned up a couple of weeks later, and the procedure was repeated, although the coffee break was slightly abbreviated. The same room was requested, and by good fortune for them (alas, poor occupancy levels for me) it was available. Three hours later, off they went with the identical excuse!

The money was very welcome, and it was always cash. It meant that we could service the room and re-let it again that same evening, should we be lucky enough to have prospective occupants. After the third visit – yes, same excuse once again – they never came back. Did they fall out, did they get found out, or were they too embarrassed to pull the same old trick? I never did find out.

Another strange going-on featured a large black gentleman who came to the hotel once a week on a particular day, for a couple of months or so.

The reservation and payment had been made by a lady who always arrived in advance of the gentleman, who was broad of shoulder and trim of waist. All of a flutter she was, presumably in anticipation of the arrival of the said gentleman. In he would stroll, muscles rippling from what must have been his regular workouts. After a pot of coffee to maintain the decencies, they would repair upstairs to their bedroom and would not be seen again for a number of hours until they would rush downstairs looking at their respective watches and flying out through the front door. A squeal of tyres and a revving engine signalled their hurried departure.

It was not until towards the end of their run of visits that I plucked up the courage to ask them what was going on. I thought that I had woven my query rather adroitly into a brief conversation with them. It transpired that the aforesaid gentlemen had to return whence he came in order to check in at evening roll-call. These stays at my hotel were officially classed as "conjugal visits" and the gentleman was on day-release from an open prison, with his term of full-time incarceration coming towards an end. I had mistakenly thought that the idea of day release was to assist in the rehabilitation of a convicted offender into normal day to day society. How wrong I was – it seems it was for the sole purpose of exercising conjugal rights!

But who was I to take issue with such a forward-thinking government initiative? I was so pleased to have been able to play such a pivotal part in his rehabilitation into society. I wonder what became of him, and hope that he is now an upright pillar of the community.

Chapter 8

Friends and Neighbours

I loved my dogs. It was impossible to imagine life without that close bond to hand. It's truly something special to enjoy the love that seeps from every pore of your canine partner.

My adult life with dogs had started with Becket, who sat in the car with me, covering over 30,000 miles a year. Then came Midge, a long-legged Border terrier, followed on by Moss, her daughter. They meant the world to me and saw me through dark times, asked so little but gave me so much. Midge had a litter of six and I ensured that the other five went to good homes. One, whom I had named Wool because of the odd curls in his coat, went to Belgium to a wealthy family with children and a swimming pool. I hope that they all had the best of lives and still think of them, so many years later.

Though it was Becket who initially shared the space under the hotel desk in my tiny office with my feet, he never took to hotel life in quite the same way as did Midge and Moss. They were more outgoing, friendly with unknown people suddenly descending upon them, and just as suddenly disappearing again, probably not to be seen again until the following year. It must have been a strange world for them all. But in their own way, they preserved my sanity, forced me to take time out to walk with them up the lane and across the big field, and, of course, shone through with that unconditional love.

One day as my dogs and I were out walking, to our surprise we met a cow in the lane. My dogs were quite used to running around with the cows in the field. But the three of us were not used to almost bumping into a sturdy Holstein grazing placidly on the green verge of the narrow top end of the lane. On close inspection, she looked friendly and familiar, and I quickly determined that it was Beverley, and that she was an escapee from our field. Just how had she got out?

It appeared she must have simply walked out over a broken or rotten fence post, treading down the wire in between whilst blundering towards pastures new; cows are very inquisitive creatures. The dogs got quite excited as I coaxed her back through the gap and then twisted the wire into place again. Bev wandered off, without a care in the world, and was soon head down, munching away at the long grass, flicking her tail in a forlorn attempt to swat away the flies from around her eyes and nether regions.

I knew the repair was unlikely to last very long, so proper remedial work was on the cards. The next morning, Nigel and I walked the boundaries and we came to the inevitable conclusion that quite a lot of work ought to be done to make the field cow-escape-proof. Some new wire and posts were ordered, and the job was put in hand as a matter of urgency. It was one thing for the locals to nod and scuttle by those cows when they were crossing the field on the public footpath, but quite another to meet one or more in the lane.

Whilst we were doing that, we decided to put a new, hardwood, five-barred gate into the corner of the field where it abutted the edge of our car park. This was a bigger undertaking because I had to hire a tractor with a huge great powered screw contraption fixed to it for drilling down into the ground in order to sink large oak posts and afterwards concrete them in before the large gate could be hung. It was rather a handsome gate, and I was quite proud of it. It would facilitate the ingress of a bigger machine into the field for the annual mowing and was to become very useful.

There was another gate that I owned, too, which was to cause all sorts of trouble.

When I had first arrived at the hotel, the lane adjacent had a large and decrepit wooden five barred gate across it, propped open, and held in place mostly by entwined ivy. Many years previously it had been painted white. Now, it just looked an eyesore which was in danger of collapse. When closed, it covered two thirds of the width of the lane, and had doubtless been purpose built many years ago to provide a token traffic barrier. The remaining third was a smaller gate, presumably for pedestrians to pass though in days of yore. It was in a similar state of decay.

It seemed odd to me, but I had quickly established from one of those junta frontagers that the gate had been erected many years previously and that once a year it must be closed to ensure that wheeled traffic did not gain the legal right to use the lane – which anyway came to a dead end after about half a dozen houses. Something to do with old easements and rights of way over private property and the fact that the lane had never been adopted by the authorities.

Over a number of years, the large gate quietly mouldered away further and nobody came by to close it. So, after about five years, I decided that I would do so, hopefully as a means of getting rid of the eyesore. After some of the larger strands of ivy were chopped away, with much creaking and groaning on rusty hinges it was persuaded to lie, semi-propped up, across the lane. I helped to keep it somewhere near vertical with an empty wooden beer barrel. Half an hour later, it could not have been longer, an outraged frontager – the same man who had told me the story of the gate – arrived in the hotel asking, without any preamble, which vandal had pulled the gate across the lane.

"And good morning indeed, to you!" I said, keeping a straight face. "I confess, t'was I!"

"Why on earth…?" he spluttered.

"But you specifically indicated that it must be closed on one day of the year in order to comply with and maintain that bye-law you were so keen on. I decided that today is the day to re-enact the ceremony!"

"But… but… I can't get out!" He was verging on the apoplectic.

"But is not that the whole idea? On this one day a year, there is to be no passage of motor traffic. You told me that yourself!"

"Don't be so bloody stupid! Go and move it out of the way!"

"My dear sir, if you want it moved, then you will have to do it yourself. I am not going to be liable for breaking a long-standing bye-law. Heaven only knows what trouble I could land myself in." I added with a mumbled aside, "Particularly with you lot."

Off he stamped and moved first the barrel and then the gate, breaking it as he did so, as I had suspected would happen. Later in the day, we went out and heaved all the rotten wood away and piled it up alongside the remains of the old garage-cum-fire-station. The matter was never mentioned to me again, so I assumed that nobody was really that bothered about maintaining their rights, particularly if it meant putting their hands into their own pockets.

The smaller gate was an old design of a miniature five-barred gate with a rather attractive triangular upstand on top. And he did come back a week or two later to mention the smaller gate. What was I going to do with it? One side of it was attached to the wall outside the hotel, so he deemed it my responsibility.

Across the centre of the gate was attached a painted sign stating that the lane was private property, for the use of frontagers only and naming the properties, and for their guests only. There was, in addition, a pedestrian right of way along the lane, which led out at the far end to a council estate. The gate itself was in poor condition, and the painted sign even more so, with the weather having obliterated most of the lettering over the years. I decided that I would take over responsibility for the maintenance of the gate, because it was a nice old feature, and was probably part of village history, as no doubt had been its bigger brother, now consigned to history.

So, having pondered, I wrote a lovely letter to all of those living up the lane, inviting them to share between them the cost of putting up a new sign, to be beautifully painted, and providing an estimate of the work required. In return for their shared payment, I agreed that I would be responsible henceforth for repair, regular maintenance and painting of the actual gate. That seemed a fair division to me.

Not one single person living along that lane was prepared to put their hand in to their pocket and stump up a very modest amount of money to maintain their sign on what was originally probably their gate. So, I took down their sign and painted the gate a lovely glossy white. And, of course, nobody said another word either about the missing signage or about the big gate either, which was never replaced. Strange stuff, is it not, when people (all of considerable means) are asked to put their hands in their pockets for the local or common good?

My son Marcus was growing into a fine strapping lad. I spent much less time with him in his early years than I would have liked, but that was the business that I was in, and it provided well for my family over his growing years.

Although he had been at boarding school, Marcus would fit easily back into the hotel when he was on holiday, helping out where needed. For a number of years, he was on the Christmas roster for the restaurant, helping to serve up to fifty covers at Christmas lunchtime. No complaints – he just buckled down to it, all being part of hotel life as he and I knew it.

By the age of seventeen, he was desperate for a set of wheels of his own, so I bought him an old refurbished Series III Land Rover for his birthday. I acquired it from Dunsfold Land Rovers, nationally known for refurbished machines. This particular Series III had been fitted, at my request, with a new galvanised chassis – they all rotted through at some stage – and various other tweaks such as free wheel hubs, to provide an easier drive on the public roads, whilst still maintaining the legendary off-road capability. It looked super-smart in green with a cream rear top and black interior seats. I parked it outside the hotel, and I shall never forget the look on Marcus' face when I handed over a key and he realised that it was for him. The Land Rover was an important and very welcome milestone in his life just then. It soon disappeared in the direction of university, where I imagine it became regularly overloaded with student friends.

I taught him the rudiments of driving it in the big field by the hotel, where we bounced around, and made liberal use of the four-wheel drive characteristics for which Land Rovers are rightly famous. It brought out the local junta of grumbly locals; of course it did. There was a bit of low key "What's going on here then?" to which the inevitable reply was along the lines of "Mind your own business, please."

Driving a Land Rover around one's nine-acre field seemed to me to be an eminently acceptable activity, even if there were rather a large number of clashed gears as learning progressed.

Later I took him to a disused aerodrome, where we managed to get ourselves on to the old and scarred runway system, last used in anger in World War Two as a fighter or bomber base. Round and round we went, still with the occasional clashing of gears, but Marcus was learning, always learning. He passed his driving test at the first attempt, which was better than I had managed to achieve. I failed because I didn't brake for the "pretend" emergency stop when the examiner hit the dashboard with his clipboard. In my defence, we were on a busy dual carriageway at the time, and it was nearly half an hour since he had told me of that instruction, which I had by then completely forgotten.

On a couple of occasions whilst I was walking my dogs round the big field there were a couple of shifty looking blokes grasping metal detectors which they waved to and fro in front of them as they walked about. Being a polite and laid-back sort of individual, I wandered over with the dogs and greeted them. In surly fashion, we were barely acknowledged. The dogs' hackles went up. They knew a bad 'un when they saw one.

"What are you doing, then?" I asked. As if it wasn't obvious.

"Detecting. What does it look like?" said one of them with a surly nod towards the devices.

"Oh, what for?" I asked.

"Why?" Their eyes slid sideways from one to the other.

"Well, I'm interested, that's why." This was going nowhere fast, I could see.

"What's it to you, then?" Their tone was getting more aggressive.

"Well, do you have permission from the owner? This is, after all, private property."

"So, what are you doing here then?"

"Aha! It's my field, you see, and my hotel over there, so I do have a reasonable right to ask you. I think that you had better go."

They didn't like that at all, and things then went further downhill when they stood their ground and I threatened to call the police. They countered with the suggestion of damaging a few cars in the car park. Discretion being the better part of valour – and there being two of them, both of them larger and younger – the dogs and I beat a tactical retreat.

I wished that I had not been so foolish as to have mentioned ownership of the hotel, and I was a tad nervous for a few days, but, thanks be, I never saw them again. They were not local people, from their accents, so how had they come across that particular field?

When I had first put cows on it, the locals were soon up in arms and said that they were terrified to walk across the field on the little tarmac (public) footpath. They were country people, for heaven's sake! I eventually gave in by moving the cows away and replacing them with half a dozen horses. There were no local complaints over that, but a number of hotel guests would not cross that field for fear of I don't know what.

One couple from London told me that the field was heaving with snakes, and nothing would get them to go back in. Strange people, those city dwellers. I never could get the hang of them.

"The field!" they said, huffing and puffing as they ran back into the hotel. "Snakes!" puff, puff, "Everywhere!"

"Oh, really?" said I. "The bar is open, just go through there and have a stiff one to get over it."

That great field was near to the centre of our village, so it was unsurprising that one year a small delegation of local people arrived on the hotel doorstep.

"Welcome, welcome! Do come in. Have you come for lunch?" I was pleased to see fresh local people darkening my doorway.

"Erm, no. Erm... we were wondering if it might be possible to have the village bonfire on your big field?" The poor chap was almost tugging at his forelock. I thought that he might even bow at one stage.

"Yes, of course! Why not? I would be delighted – it's the least that we can do to help out!"

"Yes, well, thank you, but what about the animals, then?"

"I'm sure that it will be no problem." I said, "I'll arrange for them to go away on holiday for a few days to a local farm." I knew that one of my regulars would oblige. "Just let me know which day that you want to kick off with building it."

More tugging of forelocks before they beat a hasty retreat to save them shelling out for even a coffee.

Yes, of course, I was delighted. Closer links with people in the village could only be a bonus, because a small number of them still saw me as a bit of an interloper. Nevertheless, I made a point of telling them that there had to be a complete clearance, preferably the next day, because of the horses, which would be returning to their usual field.

It's that age-old thing of nobody speaking to you unless you have lived there for at least twenty-five years. Most people knew exactly who I was, as it was no secret, and I was an employer of local people. But despite that, every single day, I would walk my dogs up the lane and through the kissing gate into the field to give them some exercise, and there would usually be some local person that would fail to react to my cheerful morning greeting.

Small village life – and the village inhabitants – could be a pain sometimes.

But the bonfire should ease the situation, I thought. A few days before the date, I arranged for the horses to go to the farm at the other end of the village. Villagers arrived with all sorts of wood, old mattresses, broken cupboards and the like, and soon there was a really impressive stack of stuff ready for the great day. The pile looked like one of those huge beacons that the Saxons would have erected and lit up to warn of a Viking invasion. The day turned out to be dry but bitterly cold, and as soon as the festivities got going, I realised that I had utterly missed a trick. Why had I not thought to be offering hot punch or something like that? At least it would have paid my waitresses' wages that night. As it was, they were just twiddling their thumbs with nothing to do.

No matter, it was all great fun, apart from the fact that some idiot had authorised the setting up of the firework display very close to our car park, so someone had to be detailed by me to keep an eye on things lest a spent rocket landed on a guests' car. I was sure that the fantastic bonfire, blazing skywards, could have been seen for miles, right across the valley. It was a grand night out for the village children, and indeed for the rest of us.

The next morning, a couple of locals could be seen quartering the field to pick up litter and sticks from fired rockets and the detritus of cans and bottles. It didn't seem to take them long. Others put back the turf that they had lifted in advance from under the position of the bonfire. In the afternoon, I went with the dogs and picked up what they had missed. To my disgust, I filled at least a couple of big black bin bags.

Oh, and nobody took the trouble to come to thank me.

The following year was much the same, and the clearance was no better. Yet again there were no thanks. I told the organisers that we had ourselves picked up a couple of large black bin bags full of litter and used fireworks after they had done their job. My problem was that I could not bring cows – or the horses that I had by then – back into the field with bits of plastic left around for them to ingest.

My polite remonstration obviously fell on deaf ears. I dumped the full bags with one of the organisers and gave them fair warning that if it happened again, that would be it.

Still no thanks, three years on the trot. Should I really have expected any?

Sure enough, the following year saw a veritable pile of stuff still left in the field, despite half a dozen people walking about afterwards. Was I prepared to risk the life and expense of a horse ingesting lumps of plastic? No. So that was that, and I fired off a letter to the organisers saying that the field would not be available the following year. No thanks, not even an answer to the letter.

My popularity went down a peg or two for a while.

Chapter 9

Are Chefs worth their Salt?

We had a succession of cooks and chefs over the years. They came and they went. Some just failed to fit in and others used us as a stepping stone to further their career. I understood and I could cope with that, because I too was pushing forwards.

As we started to get more guests to stay, and as our fledgling reputation grew, we needed to hire a cook for the evening meals. We were lucky to find a lovely lady, whose daytime job was cooking at a rather exclusive foreign school a few miles distant. She had a mantra, which I remember to this day: "Use the goodness." By that she meant that I should scrape out all of the thick gooey stuff left at the bottom of the roasting pans and swill it about with either water or (when times became better) a splash of white wine, to make a proper gravy. It's served me quite well over the years.

I judged that the time was just right for us to make the huge investment into a brand new kitchen. It had been on my list for some time, but neither funds nor progress had allowed. It would be a major leap into the unknown.

Clutching my latest set of accounts and a sort of rudimentary spreadsheet which was probably only understandable to myself, since I remained a dunce at this sort of thing, I ran it first by my accountant and then onwards to the manager at the Midland Bank, who had proved previously to be a great supporter.

Times were certainly a-changing, because on that visit he actually bought me lunch! Perhaps he felt a bit guilty about all those charges and fees that I had paid over the last few years? Lunch passed in a bit of a blur, and it was agreed that the bank would fund the new kitchen. I went straight back home and booked the builder for the job.

And what a job it was. Co-ordination between the builder, his small team, the architect who had interpreted my plan, the local planners and not least the listed building people, ran like clockwork, and soon the bare outline of the extension, built within the original footprint of the old outhouses, began to take shape, nay more than shape – it took on an identity of its own.

Blighted initially by incessant rain which saw the foundations filling with water as soon as they were dug, and bedraggled workmen seeking shelter in the old kitchen, from which they were immediately expelled, progress faltered until the new moon brought blessed relief and called a halt to the downpours. Miraculously, then it was all plain sailing and lo and behold, a brand new kitchen was revealed behind the muddle of scaffolding and tarpaulins.

The drying out process was hastened along by the installation of what appeared to be a vast jet engine on a trolley but which was, in fact, just a commercial dryer.

Eventually, all was done, and a commercial kitchen fitting company came on site to kit it out. Plugs and three-phase wiring proved to be spot on, and before long I was able to stand in a room more akin to my idea of a spaceship. We all marvelled…

Who would take charge of this modern monster? By the mid-80s, we acquired a small brigade of kitchen personnel and more state-of-the-art machinery such as a purpose-built walk-in cold-room, imported, sad to say, from Germany. A huge extractor fan took away any odours before they could permeate into the other parts of the building, driven out through a venting system which itself cost a small fortune. It was all a wonder to behold, and I was rather proud of it.

My mother wandered in when it was first opened for business, looked around her, and retreated, shaking her head.

"What on earth is all that stuff for?" she enquired.

"Well, we couldn't go on as we were. You know that we have to move with the times, and be prepared to do more business. It has taken months to build this brand-new kitchen on to the side of this old building, what with getting planning permission, a builder to actually turn up and do the work, and then to kit it all out. This way, I'm going to be ahead of the game and it should stand us in good stead for the future."

"Huh! I liked it just as it was."

"Mother! The old kitchen was a poky little hole, and I couldn't ask trained professional kitchen staff to work in it. They would just laugh at me and do a runner!"

Mind you, grand though it was, I still retained a soft spot for that old kitchen and the basic old-fashioned household cooker – it was where it had all started for me and I was quite sentimental about it all for quite some time.

As business improved, everything was ploughed back and that was when I decided to buy the conservatory to be erected on the back of the building. This would provide us with a meeting room, or a coffee shop, or overflow from our dining room, which was now known, more pretentiously, as a restaurant. It had a rather pretentious name as well, The Camelia Restaurant, named after the lovely tree in the garden right outside. Because of the plants that we put in the new conservatory, my mother liked to refer to it as "The Orangery".

Planning permission for the conservatory was, for once, non-contentious. Tucked out of the way right at the rear of the main building, there were no local objections and nor did the planners seem to have any problem with it. Mind you, we were going for a top of the range model, with a low brick surround up to, say, hip height, and then large glass panels on the sides and the roof. No plastic was to be involved, and all the framework was to be in seasoned hardwood.

When the conservatory was up and running, stocked with commercial cane furniture and pretty, dark green patterned Romo fabrics, we started off by using it for breakfasts instead of using the restaurant. In that way the tables could be laid up for breakfast the evening before. But when winter came along, we soon decided that the conservatory was not going to be at all popular. I spotted the morning waitress walking around in a fleece jacket!

"Too cold in there, first thing, sir!"

Glass conservatories suffered the perennial problem of being too hot in summer, and too cold in winter. Roof blinds had to be installed in order to try to keep in some overnight heat, and extra panel heaters had to be fitted along the side walls. Then it became our newest venture, a coffee shop, and one of the part-timers that lived locally made fabulous Dundee cakes and the like for us. It went quite well, and we expanded to doing light lunches in there.

The next problem to raise its ugly head concerned my posh new Ladies and Gents, built adjacent to the conservatory. The brass fittings were immediately misunderstood as being gold, and brought forth many a ribald comment.

People would traipse in to the hotel, trying to look as though they knew where they were going, and would end up in the new loos. Then they would walk straight back out of the hotel without so much as a thank you.

It may seem pernickety, but when usage of your loos has been repeatedly abused, day after day for months and months, you start to see red. One day, I jumped up from the front desk, fuming.

"Don't do it!" said Carol, looking up from her typewriter and clearly rather nervous at my pent-up head of steam.

"No, enough is enough," I grumbled through clenched teeth. And then into battle I went. A few times I asked if they would like to make a small contribution to a charity to offset my costs. Once or twice I rattled a charity tin that had been left with us. They just looked at me as though I was a lunatic and passed on by. I really couldn't believe it! Once, some blighter even had the cheek to nick the charity tin from the front desk!

What was even worse was the number of those people who took away the toilet rolls with them when they left. Not just the spare one, but the one in use as well, and the soap and other ladies' stuff, particularly if they were walkers using the nearby country trails. How mean is that?

The first I realised about that particular problem was when a gentleman sidled up to us at reception and asked, *sotto voce*, if the ladies' loo could be re-supplied with "the necessaries" as a matter of some urgency. His dear wife found herself to be in a somewhat compromising situation, but just how had she communicated with him? When you have had half a dozen loo rolls nicked on just one Sunday, it really is time to draw the line.

"My dear sir, I cannot apologise enough to you. A member of staff will be with your dear lady wife in two shakes of a cats' tail."

An hour later, we had to do it all over again.

Meanwhile, with the inauguration of the new kitchen, it had become the right time to hire a full-time chef with proper qualifications and a checkable CV. We also needed someone who would fit in with the rest of our happy band, so personality was important too.

We found the right person in Keith and he came with the added bonus of his wife, Lily. They had both been working at a small but well-known hotel in the Cotswolds and thought that it was time to move on to somewhere which they understood might offer more promise. Keith was a good chef and made himself instantly at home in the new kitchen, and Lily moved herself seamlessly into the office behind reception and thoroughly reorganised me, much to my chagrin because I could not find things anymore, not understanding her modern systems. She was super-efficient, however, and really good with the guests.

Keith started us down the road towards gaining food awards from the AA, those famous and coveted Rosettes. For some time, I had been having thoughts about how respected merit awards from outside companies might bring in extra revenue and put us further on the map, and here was a prime example which now could be within our grasp. By the following year, with his help, we achieved 1 Rosette status. Our food improved immeasurably under the careful eye of Keith and the AA Rosette was a just reward for his efforts. I never did find out who the inspector was that checked us out and recommended us for that initial award. However, I decided to make it my business for the future to learn about and hopefully identify hotel inspectors when they came to me. I learned something from others in the business, which was to prove important and very useful and that was "know your inspectors". That was going to prove vital as time went by, and I became a dab hand, envied by other hoteliers around us.

Keith and Lily stayed for nearly three years, and I was really sorry when they left us for pastures new and to further progress their careers. If they had been just a bit older, and I had been a bit more business savvy, I would have been well served to offer them a small slice of partnership in the business, but it was not right just then because my domestic personal arrangements were rocky at that point, to say the least.

Next came Robin, a very talented chef – so young, but with so much latent talent, almost bursting out of him. Unfortunately, he had a very aggressive mother, who would telephone both him and me during working hours for no necessary reasons. Robin would go on to make a name for himself in due course elsewhere. But for now, he suited well, and improved easily and quickly on what had gone before.

Our 1 Rosette was never likely to be in doubt on his watch and, indeed, it was with him that the coveted 2 Rosettes were first achieved. To be fair, he worked his socks off, but his timekeeping left something to be desired. It really was no good turning up at one minute to eight in the morning if service was to begin at eight on the button.

"Oh, come on. It's not a problem. I was here on time. I left everything ready last night. All they had to do for me was lay it out, turn on the stove and away we go." This was his reasoning that he rolled out on far too many occasions.

"What happens if someone wants to get away early?" I asked.

"We don't start till eight!"

"No, not so, we would try to accommodate their wishes."

"Why? They know the score."

"Oh, and what happens if your car breaks down, or you have a puncture?"

"But it hasn't!"

That sort of attitude was not helpful and I was having to turn up ready to do breakfasts on a just-in-case basis, because the breakfast waitress or waiter would invariably ring me at my cottage over the other side of the lane when panic set in as it got near to eight o'clock and they could see or hear early guests making their way towards the restaurant. It was unacceptable because not only was I having to do part of his shift, but it lengthened my working day quite a lot.

Robin would obviously bleat to his mother when he got home, because she was in the habit of yelling at me down the telephone, far too often for my liking. I thought that she was a bit bonkers. In the end I put the phone down on her after one particularly long diatribe, having told her quite succinctly that I neither employed her nor paid her salary, and was therefore not prepared under any circumstances to discuss a staff member with her, even if it was her adult son.

The writing was on the wall when Robin asked to sit down with me and told me that we should be aiming for 3 Rosettes. I looked at him in some confusion.

"I know that I can get us there," he said.

"No, Robin, I don't think that's a good idea."

I was confused. I had sat him down on a number of occasions to try and make it clear that the general prosperity of the hotel did not just lie within his kitchen domain. Centres of profit were interlinked and needed to provide a harmonious whole in order to result in an end of year profit sufficient to continue the investments required in upgrades and modernisation – and not least to be able to pay all the wages and bonuses. I firmly believed that should we achieve 3 Rosettes, then everything would have to change. People would beat a path to our door for a 2 Rosette meal, and even more should, in theory, come for 3 Rosettes. But they would be different people, with much higher expectations. Prices would have to rise, extra staff would be needed with higher levels of skills, and my accommodation pricing structure would sit uncomfortably with the price bracket in which we would then have to trade. No, I didn't want another of those Rosettes. I believed that I knew my niche in my particular marketplace by now.

"But I am absolutely sure that I can do it," argued Robin.

"Yes, that's as maybe. I expect that, in a couple of years, we might reach three. But I don't want three Rosettes. Ever!"

Such a talent, but he was not prepared, or even able, to see the other side of the coin.

Two AA Rosettes fitted nicely into my marketing and into guest expectations. More to the point, if a chef was off, I could step into the breach at that level with a certain degree of confidence. If I had to train upwards, no, I had neither the time nor the inclination. I knew my limitations when it came to that.

Another young man to join the kitchen brigade was Dan. He just turned up one day and asked me for a job. He looked so scruffy that I had no idea at first how he had wheedled his way past my gatekeeper Carol. But he possessed an infectious smile and when tested, demonstrated that he knew his way around a kitchen, having worked in a number of pubs. He felt it was time to move on, and I felt that he needed a change, albeit only part-time because of other commitments.

"Can I speak freely to you, young man?" I asked rather tentatively.

"OK."

"Well, go away and give yourself the wash and brush up of your life, if you want a trial. Don't be offended, but you need a haircut and some better clothes. I can't have people working here that look as though they have fallen through a hedge."

"Shall I start tomorrow, then? I'd better get back to my mum and give her the good news!"

And with that he was gone, leaving me rather bemused at how easily I had caved in. But, yes indeed, there he was on the morrow, freshly scrubbed and hardly recognisable. He fitted in rapidly and almost took over the breakfast rota, which suited everyone.

Dan was to remain part-time but was very good at his job – when he worked – and had a beat-up old banger of a car that had probably never been near a MOT centre for years. Inevitably, it eventually died on him, and he said that he couldn't afford to buy another one, so would be unable to continue to come to work with us. Despite all that, he could have made something of himself in the kitchen, particularly if he could be persuaded to give us more shifts, so I thought that it would be worth stumping up for another old banger for him, and so I did. Unfortunately, I didn't think it through properly and put it into his name, not mine. Perhaps over a year later, Dan and the car left late one evening after his shift had ended, never to be seen again.

Years later, I found myself in a similar situation where I had to buy another car for another chef. This time it was a small used Volvo which had to be bought quickly to replace the similar model that he had totalled on the way in to do breakfast service one icy morning. Why I should have concluded that such was my fault, I cannot recall. But buy the car I did, in order to maintain continuity of his job and my own peace of mind. This time I was just a bit cannier; I got my money back through deductions from his salary, only moving the car over to his ownership once he had paid me back in full.

The worst thing that could happen – apart from not turning up at all – was for one of the chefs to turn up for his shift the worse for wear. Fortunately, I had a good brigade in the kitchen, and it did not happen very often. There was only one course of action, and that was to send him or her straight home; if it was a busy night, you can imagine the possible mayhem with all those sharp knives being wielded about. In such circumstances it was time for me to roll up my sleeves and get stuck in to service with the rest of them, dusting off my half-forgotten skills of yesteryear.

Pink with the exertion, I looked back on those emergency shifts and realised that, despite everything, I had rather enjoyed myself.

I picked up a mantra from one of my chefs. He was training a young lad to become his commis chef and was supervising a particular dish that they had produced together. After wiping the plate round the edges so that there would be no finger marks on it he came up with the following comment:

"With every plate that goes out with your name on it, laddie, remember that you should be proud to be serving it to your mum on her birthday. If it's not good enough for her on her special day, then it's not good enough to be served here."

I rather liked that.

Chapter 10

Difficult Suppliers

I am very fond of cheese. Cheese, however, is not good for gout. I must therefore carefully tread the middle ground throughout my life so as to enjoy the one but to banish the recurrence of the other. It is a tightrope from which I occasionally fall, extremely painfully.

I never thought that I would fall out with a purveyor of cheeses, though.

The tale goes as follows. We were very proud of the fact that we were able to offer our guests an extensive and well-informed cheeseboard to complete and complement their meal. A modest array of well-known and speciality cheeses could be sampled, and we had dealt with a particular supplier for some time. Staff were well rehearsed in names, types, and taste of what was on the cheeseboard. I sometimes wondered if they didn't nibble more than the paying customers, such was their diligence in pursuit of knowledge.

Robin the troublesome chef decided to change the existing arrangement without consulting me, and different cheeses started to appear in the restaurant. I had no initial problem with that; but there did become a problem when the first monthly invoice from a new supplier crossed my desk. I did not recognise the cheese company letterhead, but more importantly, nor did I like the prices that appeared on the invoices that kept fluttering on to my desk. Everything seemed to be costing just that little bit too much, and like a mouse, it was nibbling away into my profit margin.

I bided my time, and a week or so thereafter, a large green refrigerated van pulled up right outside the front door, emblazoned with the name and logo of that new cheese supply company. I gave it a couple of minutes and then tootled outside. My chef Robin was already deep in the bowels of the van, chatting animatedly with the driver.

I climbed the rear steps, and hauled myself upwards and entered the van with its racks of cheeses on display, nodding to the driver, who clearly had no idea who I was – indeed why should he? I started to look through some of the produce on offer, clutching the invoice in my hand, behind my back. The word "furtive" came instantly to mind as I listened in to the deep discussions between my chef and the driver, with both of them casting glances in my direction. Something underhand was clearly going on. I asked to try a couple of cheeses, ones that we were now stocking. I asked about prices where they were not listed, and the penny quickly dropped. The prices on the cheeses, before any discount, were higher on my invoice. I was being skimmed!

"Very nice selection you have here." I nodded in the direction of the van driver.

"Yes, thanks. I'll be with you in a minute when I have finished with this gentleman."

Chef was looking decidedly uncomfortable by this time, and it must have communicated itself to the driver.

"What?"

"I don't think that we will be continuing the account for this hotel." I said mildly to the driver.

"Oh, no, really, and who might you be then?" He said, his voice raised in anger.

"Well, I'm actually the chap who has been paying your bill," I said. "But there will be no more, because please don't go out of your way to come back here again!"

There was the inevitable brief slanging match, not helped by the guilty looks passing between the chef and the driver, as justification was attempted and singularly failed. I ended it by telling him that he had thirty seconds to get off my driveway or I would be calling his head office. Chef and I jumped out from the back of the van and he departed in haste, kicking up a spray of my neatly raked gravel as he hurtled down the drive, never to be seen again.

Chef and I went inside the hotel. I think that he must have felt my gaze burning onto the nape of his neck.

"I know you must be busy now, Chef, but please find the time to come and see me at the end of your shift. We need to have a little talk."

But what, really, was there left to say? I don't like being done over by my own staff. Marching orders were drawn up in my mind, even though not yet actually issued. But the time was coming…

The breakup actually did come soon after. He misbehaved once too often and, in the end, he had to go. I was not sorry. He went to a large nationally known country house hotel in the West Country where his talents might have fitted in with a larger brigade. I never heard from him or about him again.

After Robin came a long period of calm, with a new chef, locally based, who could maintain our two Rosettes with a bit of support, but, unless I malign him, could not ever have got to the magic three.

That suited both of us just fine.

Food costs account for one of the largest single areas of expense in any hotel, after staffing has been taken into account. The head chef was responsible for spending a lot of my money, on his own authority, but a tight check needed to be kept.

I needed every chef that I employed to be able to cost the produce that he was in charge of ordering and let me have notes of what he was going to put on to our regularly changing menu together with the itemized cost per meal, so that I could ensure that we charged out to the public at a reasonable profit, whilst keeping prices in check. We often had to work in reverse. I told the chef what we were going to charge for our meals, whether *table d'hôte* or à *la carte*, and it was up to him to work his costs so that he could come up with meals within the margin that I allowed him.

Why was that so difficult for them? So many struggled to offer reliable and consistent costings. I got used to having to check rough scrawls of figures that made little or no sense. In the end, I adapted to the inevitable and did it myself, but it would make me very cross when I checked through a butcher's or greengrocer's delivery invoice halfway through each morning.

I would pop my head in through the kitchen and ask the chef of the moment to join me in the office.

"Why did you order that, then?" I would ask, to be met by a glum silence, with him not meeting my eye. "Did you know how much it was going to cost when you ordered it?"

The answer was always, "I don't know" or, "Err, no, sorry about that."

Heaven help me, but why on earth did they think that they were going to get away with it, and why did they not learn in the first place?

"Well, tell them to uplift it when they come in the morning. It is out of season and frankly a silly price."

"Err, well, I can't do that because I've got it on the menu tonight. Oh, and unless you want me to offer frozen peas, I have no appropriate back up."

No back up? Words just failed me. What was that blasted new walk-in cold room for then?

Why could chefs not order things that were in season in glorious England rather than opting to buy (with my money!) stuff that had to travel most of the way round the world from some country where the labourers are paid almost slave wages to grow and harvest it? To make it worse, it is usually quite tasteless as well as being ridiculously expensive.

The only altercation I had with our trusted gardener, Nigel, was when I told him that his beloved vegetable patch was going to be slabbed over to make a terrace, and that there were to be two garden-facing downstairs bedrooms at the back, suitable for disabled guests. It was quite the thing to be able to tell people that we grew our own vegetables, and the patch was quite extensive, probably seventy yards long by half that wide. As we got busier, though, it was a pointless exercise. Everything that we grew would be used up so quickly, and the new stuff had no chance to mature before we were off to the local market to supplement our requirements. Nigel put in a couple of rows of peas, and was a little put out to find that I had munched my way through the entirety of both rows without a pod having reached the kitchen.

Suppliers, meanwhile, continued to be the bane of my life. I had, in my ignorance, thought that they should be pleased to supply us with their goods and services, in exchange for which I would pay them correctly and on time.

Things never seemed to work out exactly like that.

The problem originally seemed to lie at my mother's door. I learned that for the first couple of years, she had been in the habit at Christmas of inviting them into the hotel and giving them a drink, a mince pie and a huge tip for deigning to provide their service during the last year. In addition to the tip, bottles of scotch would also be liberally spread about. And then my parents wondered why there was no profit! It was probably a throwback to days gone by, as my mother would have been used to servants in her family home when she was young.

I well remember my second Christmas there at the hotel, when those poor suppliers must have wondered whether they had suddenly entered into a parallel universe as they queued up outside the back door to the old kitchen. I politely suggested to one and all that there would be no largesse flowing from the hotel, but rather, should they wish to continue to provide us in the coming year, then they might care to offer their thanks in advance by guaranteeing better prices for the coming year and by giving us a Christmas bonus. I was not popular at all, but one of them did say to me rather grudgingly that they all realised that that particular gravy train had to hit the buffers one day, and it was only a question of when.

From the beginning, I tried hard to use local suppliers and in particular for bread, fish and meat. It would be many years before we started to make our own bread, and at the onset the local delivery lady from the next village would arrive at the back door each mid-morning, and we would take from her whatever our needs would be. It was a fairly regular and standard order, and it served us well for a number of years. Sliced white loaves, and a few rolls to go with the soup at lunchtime and dinner were the order of the day.

I did not like the lady personally, but that was irrelevant. She seemed to think that she was doing us the favour, whilst I thought it should be the other way around. We clearly just rubbed each other up the wrong way. The arrangement eventually fell over because of brown bread. She didn't stock it on her van, and we decided that it was an option that had to be offered to our guests. So, she got some on board, but then muddled up between the two colours, and when we did not take a specified number of loaves for a few days running – probably due to bad weather – the sparks started to fly. I filled a freezer with bread that we didn't want, to try to keep the peace, but when she got abusive, I cancelled everything and went elsewhere. It was my first black mark in village relations.

There was a small fish counter at the back of the village grocer's shop, presided over by a large elderly lady who offered a very limited selection of fish, and often could not supply either the quantity or the quality required. Smoked haddock was always of the painted variety and stuff such as scallops were a complete no-no, but I still bought most of my fish from her, such as whiting. In those days whiting was usually served twisted around in a circle so that the tail was held in place by the head. Odd, or what?

Kippers were on the breakfast menu – not those horrible painted fillets but real whole kippers. The problem was that they were generally huge; far too big for a delicate breakfast plate. I am very partial to a kipper or two, and the best without doubt are Manx. Things came to a head with our village supplier when we ordered some boxes of Manx kippers from a wholesaler whom I had discovered, which were delivered overnight in wooden boxes at the back door to be brought in by the first person to come on duty. And they were significantly cheaper for a much better product! Villagers being villagers, it was quite soon that the dear lady at the fish counter heard about it and took personal affront. So much so that, when I hove before her one day she let fly with a venomous tirade of abuse – right in front of a shop full of people – telling me that I should be supporting local business to the exclusion of all other. That was the very last day I ever went into that shop. Black mark number two.

The supply of meat was another case in point. There were two butchers' shops in the village, and I rather favoured one over the other, though I made sure to hand out trade to both, if a little unevenly. As we got busier, we clearly needed to purchase more meat and at better prices. One shop would deliver, but the other one would not or could not. So that was that for one of them. But pricing became an issue.

One day, or rather night I should say, I went down to Smithfield market in London, and at about three o'clock in the morning I was traipsing around huge wholesaler stands trying to get a deal for a regular supply. I wondered what on earth I was doing because I had literally no clue as to how to proceed as I wandered along the aisles of the huge market where sides of beef and every other imaginable animal were being butchered whilst everyone seemed to be shouting at the tops of their voices. Half a dozen times I was almost run down by huge meat trolleys, before I plucked up the courage to ask a friendly-looking face how to proceed.

Yes, he could put a whole rolled sirloin of beef on to the early morning train to our local station. We exchanged information over a cup of extremely strong tea in a café at the end of the market. He wanted to know the likely size of orders, and the number of covers in our restaurant, stuff like that.

"Just ring me the day before, and we will get it to you," he said. What a trusting man.

"What about payment?" I asked.

"Monthly invoice." He was clearly a man of few words.

"Quite sure?" We had only just met. I too could be

monosyllabic. The deal was sealed with a handshake and he rushed off back into the tumult that was the market.

There was no problem, all those years ago, in getting a case of meat put onto the train in London, which would arrive into our local station at about seven in the morning. The often-bloody carton, containing the likes of a whole boned and rolled sirloin of beef, chuck steak, ox kidney and various cuts of lamb and pork, would be heaved out onto the platform, and I would find it parked on a bench and cart it away back to the hotel. I cannot imagine that being allowed nowadays, with no docket to be signed before I uplifted it. Yet again, the rumour mill rampaged through the village, and my butchers in the village made their displeasure quietly known.

But what was I to do? I could buy that beef a great deal cheaper than they could supply it to me, and the same went for all the other stuff that I got from London over the phone. That was my third black mark in the village, and there was an uneasy truce for a number of months, helped on my side by the fact that I was by then employing, either full- or part-time, a good half dozen local people. It all blew over eventually, of course, as people realised that I needed to buy competitively in order to keep costs down and drive business forward. I kept on using both of the local butchers for small orders when we ran short, but I never went into that fish shop ever again, nor dealt with the abusive bread lady.

It's strange how things go around over a period of years. By the time we had two AA Rosettes under our belt, the watchword in the industry was to use local produce wherever possible, and it was something that we embraced where we could. By then, our trading orders were that much bigger, and, for example, the wholesale greengrocer – who had a retail shop too – in a nearby town was happy to deliver to us three mornings a week despite a round trip of thirty miles or so. It prompted them to do business at other hotels on the route, so everyone was happy. Meat arrived on a refrigerated van from a similar distance, and by then we made all of our own bread.

Peace was to reign in the camp at last!

Chapter 11

Special Guests

The hotel was a rather photogenic property, and one of the useful and profitable spin-offs was being visited by celebrities and even film companies looking for new and unexposed properties to feature in films, advertising or the like.

The BBC wanted to book us completely for a particular project. An enthusiastic letter landed on the mat one day, stating the range of dates required. I wrote back with my prices, suitably discounted for a block booking. A letter came back with the OK. I then had the temerity to write again asking for a holding deposit. I knew what film companies could be like, particularly when they were covering an outside event. The star might break a leg or the weather might change, or pigs might fly, and everyone would disappear with me looking at a lot of unlettable rooms at very short notice.

A harassed lady BBC executive came on the line. "We are the BBC! We don't do deposits! We have written; surely that should be enough?"

"I'm sorry," I replied. "I simply cannot afford to take that sort of a risk. I need a fairly substantial deposit so please have a word with your bosses and get back to me quickly."

They didn't even bother to respond to me, one way or the other.

I had the same sort of enquiry from a film company making another film in a world-famous franchise.

"How many rooms do you have?" came the enquiry after opening pleasantries. I explained the set-up of doubles, twins, one single, and a couple of family type rooms, most of them, by then, en-suite.

"Yes, that seems perfect. We will take the lot. That seems just what we need. Someone will be round to look the place over and make particular arrangements for the stars. You know what they're like…"

"That sounds great. Let me know in advance when they will be coming. Please confirm to me in writing, and let's discuss a deposit by way of security."

"Sorry, but we don't work on that basis. We do have a schedule, but it can run over, and we would need to retain the rooms, or it could be cut short because the director doesn't like the weather, or whatever... I'm sure you understand?"

"Yes, of course I do, but I can't put my business at risk in that way, even for a household name."

That would have been a great publicity coup. It must take a big place to cope with that sort of business risk. Not for me, though. And that was the end of that.

But that didn't stop a list of famous names from beating a path up our driveway. Some came to stay, some came for lunch, some just dropped in for a coffee, or, on a memorable occasion, for afternoon tea with someone with whom he should not have been seen and who was most definitely not his spouse. Their close encounter over the cucumber sandwiches had the staff gossiping about that episode for days.

A young lady film star with a famously well-endowed *décolletage* swept into the entrance hall one morning. I was surprised that she was by herself. She just wanted coffee and her brief visit resulted in male members of staff suddenly all needing to be in the lounge for one poorly thought out reason or another. I think she was quite used to it, though, and was happy to sign some autographs for star-struck young men. A much longer stay was by an actor who stayed with us for at least a couple of weeks, rarely leaving his room, whilst he learned the lines of a new crime series on television that became hugely popular with himself in the leading role and which ran and ran for years. Lunch and dinner were served to him upstairs every day. I had absolutely no idea who he was at the time, and got quite a shock when he appeared on the screen one night!

Household names there were in abundance, mostly turning up in the sort of cars that I would covet. One such, a comedian of sorts, had a lovely new grey Ferrari with which he graced my car park, where it was nonchalantly abandoned across two spaces, and another guest, a world-famous pop star, sported an extraordinary black astrakhan overcoat that swirled around him as he twirled in the hall on his way out to an evening party, accompanied by his new wife, possibly even more well-known as part of a female pop group. Staff were once again star-struck, and so was I, on occasion. Another Ferrari, silver this time, older but far superior, was parked outside a number of times by a world-class ex-F1 racing driver, a friend of many years. He still owes me for some petrol money!

Most were gracious visitors, pleased to be able to shelter behind some much sought-after anonymity at a place where they could relax and just be themselves. Others, less so. A famous actor, part of an equally famous long running television series, yelled at me down the telephone one day when he rang for a room. "I've got a photoshoot in the next village next week, so your place will suit me perfectly. You can send the bill on to the BBC."

I instantly recognised his voice, but we were fully booked for the two nights that he required. He ranted at me mercilessly.

"Don't you know who I am?"

Oh, how I detest people that used that phrase to me. And for that he would not have got a room even if I had been able to conjure one up from thin air. What a nasty little man, I thought, even though I was an avid watcher of his series. I had always put him down as being so mild mannered.

Some readers may remember Roger Clark, who was British Rally Champion for a number of years. I knew him when I campaigned my trusty hot Ford Allardette against his Cooper S in my youth; he running with the well-known registration number 2 ANR in a series of rallies in the Midlands. He was a lot quicker than I. Many years later, amazingly, early one evening he just appeared at my reception desk. I stood and goggled, momentarily speechless.

"Good evening. Someone should have made a reservation for me for this evening. The name is Clark."

I just gaped at him across the counter. Star-struck myself for once, all I could think of to say was, "2 ANR."

He broke into a broad smile and reached out to shake my hand. When I came back to my senses, I was forced to tell him that we were fully booked and that we had absolutely no trace of his reservation. I was devastated that we were unable to look after him as I was robbed of the chance to reminisce with him. He was kindness itself and we spoke of the old days for a few brief minutes, and then he disappeared out into the night. I never saw him again, and sadly he is no longer with us.

There were plenty of other interesting guests that crossed our threshold, none more so than a loose knit group of horse racing enthusiasts. The centre of this group, and she who held it all together, was my redoubtable mother. Her brain, so seldom deployed towards the hotel, was razor sharp when it came to choosing fancied runners, the placing of bets, and the vocal enthusiasm delivered towards the television set.

My mother was a long-time fan of horse racing. It was her one abiding lifetime interest. How it all came about, I have no idea, and stupidly I never asked: it had always just been there – a part of her, and by extension, my life. But from family letters I know that she was betting on the gee-

gees well before the war. She would have a bet most days, often more than one. She had acquired a network of other racing people – trainers, assistant trainers, a number of household-name jockeys, and fellow betting enthusiasts. Visits were made by racing pundits from ITV, Channel 4 and of course the BBC; one TV pundit stayed a few times each year. Racing was my mother's only hobby, almost an addiction, but one which sadly produced little income for the hotel due to her largesse in handing out so many free drinks and meals.

I lost count of the times that one or other famous trainer would drop in to the hotel over the years, whereupon Mother would get all excited and scurry along to bend their ear. Bizarrely, it did not seem to put them off, they just came back again for more of the same. Perhaps it was those free drinks that she offered…

Her telephone network was amazing when she was trying to find the big winner of the day. There would be regular telephone calls in and out from mid-morning, whether it be for the flat or the jumps. She only used two newspapers, the *Daily Telegraph* and the *Sporting Life*. Even when she became an elderly lady, she had all her wits about her when it came to the horses, and perhaps it was a means of her keeping herself young in mind as old age continued its onward march.

I was often dragooned into taking her to a number of racecourses whilst she was hale enough to get around and enjoy the visits. There would always be someone that she knew at all the courses, and they would go into a huddle to discuss their fancied runners, often accompanied by a glass of champagne. I would be sent off to place her bets with the on-course bookie on the rails with whom she had an account. Her favourite track was Newbury, and I came to know it very well, though I was equally at home at Goodwood, Ascot, Newmarket and many others further north as far as Haydock. We usually had badges for the owners and trainers stand, kindly supplied by those friendly people in the game. She regularly made money on her bets, often substantially. Only a few times in thirty years did I have to bail her out after a heavy loss had left her racing account depleted to the point of non-existence.

One of the racers who came to stay was a fine old gentleman from Gloucester who would come to us about four times a year, for a week each time, to coincide with race meetings. Inevitably, he got to be more than a guest and became a friend. I shall always remember his face at the end of one such visit when he presented himself at reception to ask for his bill. I told him that this time it was on the house, and he was mightily pleased. One year we invited him to stay over the Christmas holiday, and naturally we didn't charge him for that either. I would reckon that he was a regular guest for almost twenty years, four times a year for a week at a time. Good business even with the odd freebie thrown in.

He drove an old Rover 105, maintained in immaculate condition, and it never let him down as far as I knew. I admired it greatly, because it was a symbol of proper British automotive craftsmanship that had completely deserted the Rover car company who by then were mass-producing inferior cars, all pretence of heritage for the marque having long gone out of the window. That Rover of his still smelt of leather and was clad in wood. It was a proper Rover.

"I know you like my old Rover," he said to me one day, as we were puttering along in it to the races. "I'll leave it to you in my Will."

I smiled at the thought, and really thought no more about it for a number of years – it could just have been a comment made in passing. I only learned later that he really had left that car to me in his Will – but it was given away to a local hospice to raise funds instead. I hoped that it made good money for the hospice and found as good a home as I would have given to it.

One couple decided to visit us for the purpose of making their own competitive analysis when we moved up to 2 AA Rosette status. They owned a nice establishment (I had seen good reports in guide book entries) about 12 miles away and saw an opportunity for checking us out. The problem was that they had obviously started out their evening on other licensed premises, and by the time they came to us they were more than just a tiny bit squiffy to put it mildly.

Every hotel receives more than their fair share of inebriated customers. Mostly, we got away with gentlemen who had taken too many pink gins before their meal and then followed them with a heavy bottle of claret during lunch or dinner. It is not easy to tactfully get across to someone that they are in dire danger of making a fool of themselves whilst not giving offence.

I had no idea who these people were until they announced loudly to everyone in the lounge that they had come for the express purposes of comparing their place to ours. They then embarked on doing a drunken sales pitch for their own hotel. It was impossible for anyone not to hear them, so I moved them up the list and got them seated in the restaurant before others who had already ordered their meals.

A bottle of wine at their table went further to their heads, with loud comments being passed about not just our food and service, but also about anyone or anything at all. As the restaurant became busier, you could have cut the atmosphere with a knife, and after they had been served with their main course, a tearful waitress came to Carol to say that she really couldn't cope with them anymore, as they had made some personal reference to her. Carol came to me and I went into the restaurant and simply asked them to leave. I cannot remember the actual words that I used, only that the sentence ended with the word "Now!"

After the usual "Well, we have never been treated like this in all of our lives," or some such, they rose from their table to muted and polite cheers from other guests. I told them that there would be no bill, and never to come back again.

In hindsight, I really should have taken their car keys away from them.

A number of months later, still in pursuit of our continued goal of my own competitive analysis, I hit on the idea of a return visit. Not out of desire for revenge, you understand, but more to see what all the fuss had been about – just how good were they, that drunken couple who had shouted the odds against us.

"Let's do it!" said my wife, ever keen to be taken out to dinner. "They won't know who I am as I wasn't there anyway when they came along. I was at home, you may remember, looking after our firstborn, with a miserable cold. You can wear a disguise and shave off your beard!"

Instead, I borrowed a pair of spectacles. Even without them, I would have made the perfect spy, with a face that could have blended into anonymity almost anywhere.

Our proposed visit had, perforce, to be at lunchtime – easier to get away for a couple of hours than in the evening.

Through nobody's fault, we came upon them on a really bad day. A lorry had chosen that morning to break down right across the entrance to their village. As we pulled up, a light tap on the passenger side window of our car heralded the arrival of the local bobby. My wife wound down her window.

"Are you trying to get to the village then, sir?" he said, smiling rather obviously at her chest area whilst addressing me.

I nodded across the footwell to him. "Yes, we are going to the hotel for lunch."

"Oh, that will be nice for you then, sir, it's a nice place." And with that he gave us directions how to get there along a nearby lane. I was glad we were in my wife's small car and not my own. After a couple of wrong turns, strangely omitted from the directions just supplied, we hove into the hotel car park, which seemed to be strangely lacking in customer cars.

"Is it closed? Did you book?" wittered my wife, seemingly worried about her free meal. She would turn up to the opening of an envelope if it was made into a social occasion.

"Don't be daft! Of course, I didn't book! The whole idea is to go incognito, isn't it! Come on, let's go in."

The whole place looked to me as though it needed a lick of paint to spruce it up. Window frames had cracked paintwork, and the front door left a lot to be desired. Strange how many hoteliers never realise that first impressions really do count.

I pushed the door open. It was as cold inside as it was outside. Nobody was about. We wandered down the hall and poked about in what was presumably the lounge, and then the dining room. Still nobody appeared. Tables were not laid up, which I thought strange.

I went back to the front desk and rang the bell on the counter again. It still had no effect.

"Hellooooo!" I shouted a couple of times, beginning to get irritated. It was like the Marie Celeste – the captain and crew had all disappeared without trace. We hung around a short while, and then gave up. Emerging from the hotel on to the car park and nearing our car, we bumped into a bloke in an old mac and wellies, pushing a wheelbarrow full of autumn leaves.

I recognised him immediately as one half of the drunken duo that had caused mayhem at my hotel. He, for his part, was giving nothing away, if he even did recognise me, which I doubted.

"Are you looking for someone?" he asked.

"Well, we had actually come here for lunch, having heard good reports about the place, but it seems to be closed. We could find nobody inside at all!"

"Ah," said the chap, "they don't open at lunchtimes, you know." What was with the 'they'? Continuing to play his part as the gardener and giving nothing away, he scratched his head as though perplexed. Perhaps he thought he recognised me after all?

And that was that. We roared off down the lane back to the main road, hoping to find a pub open. We never bothered to go back there.

With two dogs of my own, it would have been odd not to welcome pets to the hotel. We were, after all, ideally suited, having plenty of space within and without, including that large field with its bucketloads of snakes seeking to catch unwary Londoners with their poisoned fangs. I never saw even one snake in that field in 35 years. The only snake bite I ever saw was when Midge was bitten on the nose by an adder whilst snuffling in a ditch near the golf course. That did require a very rapid visit to the local vet, though I think that I was more worried about it than was Midge.

Owning an hotel in the country taught me that there were huge swathes of humanity who had actually never really been in the countryside. For them it was enough to look out of the car window on their way to yet another conurbation, enough to know that the countryside existed, without sampling its manifold delights or, heaven forbid, actually walking on unpaved land.

So, pets were very welcome, not just tolerated, and "Pets Welcome" was the name of a small and handy guide book that another hotelier down in the West Country told me about. I bought a copy and rang a few of the hotels that had taken an entry. Without exception, they gave glowing reports of increased enquiries followed by firm bookings. By what I considered to be my great good fortune, no other hotel in my county as yet had an entry, and I therefore believed that I would be able easily to convert any enquiries into bookings, particularly when I could advertise the use of that big field for their walkies.

We were a hit with that guide book from the word go. There was a regular stream of guests with their dogs (it was usually dogs) and I quickly found out a number of things:

- Just like my own, dogs are grateful animals, mostly placid and friendly.
- Their owners were even more grateful to have found a nice place to stay where their pets would be welcomed as opposed to being just tolerated – sometimes grudgingly, I was told.
- No dog ever refused to pay a bill, sought to get a discount for an alleged deficiency, or damaged the property. Well, there was one exception to that.
- However, the downside was that rooms needed extra cleaning afterwards.

That last point did not cause us any problems except in the rare case when hairs had been overlooked or a wet dog had camped out on the carpet rather than on its mat. Whilst some of us quite like the smell of wet dog – me included – I can understand that others are definitely not so appreciative.

And that damage that I mentioned? Yes, just the once. We had one lovely golden retriever that, on the first night of its stay, managed to chew through the bottom of a bedroom door whilst its owners were dining in the restaurant. An evening chambermaid, doing her rounds turning down beds, could hear a chewing and scrabbling noise, and when I was called to the scene, I was astounded to see a wet black nose peeping through a hole in the bottom of the door, about three inches from the ground. A wet tongue was flapping about in the gap. Upon being called from the restaurant, the owners were mortified, and immediately handed over more than enough cash to get the door replaced the following day. Strangely, after that solitary incident, the dog was happy to stay in the room at dinner time for the next six nights. It must have had a jolly good set of gnashers, though.

That one little guide book, which I subsequently told many fellow hoteliers about (provided that they didn't live in the same county, of course!), eventually brought in hundreds of thousands of pounds worth of income – it totted up to over ten percent of my annual turnover just before I sold in order to retire. Surely the best result ever, for a niche market?

On very rare occasions, guests brought their cats, though I could never believe that cats were in their element in an hotel environment. An elderly lady would come to stay each year, sometimes twice, with her middle-aged single daughter. The daughter had a Siamese cat which would either perch on the daughter's shoulder or walk around on a slender leather lead and was never any trouble at all. When the mother died, the daughter and the cat would continue to come for a week for a number of years. One year we never heard from them again, and that was that. I supposed that the cat had died. Or the owner.

The only other type of bird or animal that once visited us was a parrot. An African Grey it was, we were told, getting on in years, probably over 50, but it was extremely intelligent, and had mastered quite a few simple words and phrases. Nothing rude, as you might expect from exposure in *Carry On* type films, and guests and staff alike were entranced to stand and stare at it, until it spoke and they could speak back to it. I marvelled at just how intelligent other species could be.

I have always been a firm believer in sticking to one's established market, and certainly on the pet side of things, I knew we were doing the right thing, as did my dogs who got to meet new friends at the hotel every week.

One day my mother came hurtling out of her sitting room, calling out for me. She had just had a tray of tea brought to her, and I was about to go and join her for a few minutes.

"John? John! Come here quickly, John! Two dogs have just flown past my sitting room window!" She was all of a flurry.

"Dogs? What do you mean, they've flown past?" Had she started hallucinating, I worried?

"I swear that I just saw two little dogs hurtling downwards past my sitting room window!" She really was most insistent.

Mother was of a certain age by now, and charitably, one had to assume the worst when confronted by statements such as that. But she was very convinced, and after a moment or two it brought to my mind that the elderly couple who were occupying an upstairs bedroom had indeed got two dogs. Moreover, on investigation, I could see that same couple in the lounge placidly demolishing some cucumber sandwiches with their pot of Earl Grey, *sans* their dogs. So, throwing caution to the winds, I galloped outside in time to see the aforesaid two small dogs busily shaking themselves in a flower bed after having broken their fall by landing from upstairs in a large bush.

They looked at me rather sheepishly, and then cast about, wondering what they should do next. Even for them, it must have been a bit of an adventure, though they did look decidedly embarrassed.

No harm was done, other than to the immaculately topiarised bush, and the dogs were soon reunited with their owners, or "parents" as the elderly couple referred to themselves, ready for nibbles of cucumber sandwiches.

Mr S, as we shall call him, had come to stay with us for a few weeks. I seem to remember that he had business in the area, and I am sure that there was also some family connection locally. He was accompanied by a delightful golden Labrador dog, whom we all took to immediately. That dog would sit with him in the lounge in the evening, then wait there whilst he dined, being no trouble to anyone.

One night, well after dinner, there was a terrible crash in the hall, and everyone rushed to look and see what had happened. Mr S lay there at the foot of the stairs, clearly stone dead. His dog stood at the top of the staircase, gazing mournfully downwards, no doubt wondering what on earth his master was doing.

I was rooted to the spot and it was a moment or two before any reaction set in. We sent directly for the village doctor who lived close by, and he rushed round in his cardigan and slippers. He was quickly of the opinion, after an examination *in situ*, that Mr S had suffered a heart attack, causing him, as a result, to fall down the stairs. It was a quick way to go, some might say that an ending of life with such brevity was to be much sought after, but it was a great shock for those of us he left behind.

I don't think that I slept at all that night. His dog and I spent the night in the hotel lounge, welcoming the dawn chorus with a brief tour together around the car park. I was nearly run over by the sudden appearance of a large and battered Volvo estate car which ground to a halt in front of me. From the wagging of the tail of my night-time companion, I gathered that a family member had turned up.

I had nightmares about being sued by the executors of Mr S for a wobbly bannister rail (checked – no problem) or a loose bit of stair carpet (checked – no problem) or sundry other things, until the final all-clear came around. It was just as the doctor had said: he suffered a massive heart attack and was dead before he hit the bottom of the stairs.

I had offered to keep his dog, but some relatives took it away. Mr S was our first, and the Lord be praised, the only death at the hotel during my tenure.

Chapter 12

Housekeeping

As my marriage entered into a terminal stage of decline, holidays rather took a back seat until we ventured back to Tenerife, invited to stay at his apartment by a very old friend. Was it an attempt at making things work once more, perhaps as a last resort to find some common ground to see us through? If that was the case, then it failed dismally.

I cannot begin to count the number of times that I have apologised to that friend over the years for our dreadful behaviour, which culminated in the most awful of slanging matches. As he dropped us off at the airport and walked back towards his car, I imagine still the large bubble coming out from the top of his head encapsulating the words, "Thank God that's over!" How our friendship has survived continues to amaze me and he still regularly pulls my leg as we reminisce over a large Canarian measure of gin and tonic.

Soon after, my wife decided to move to a cottage in the next village. She took everything that was of importance to her, leaving nothing whatsoever behind, except for one item – her cat.

It seemed rather strange as she was inordinately fond of her cat, or so she had always said. I could only assume that there was a new partner on the scene, and perhaps he was allergic to cats?

We had all lived together in relative harmony in our little cottage, and I was quite fond of that cat, but I am a dog person, not a cat person, and there was no way that I wanted to take over responsibility for it on a full-time basis. I was away overnight from time to time, and certainly away from my cottage every day, for punishingly long hours.

When I was at home, Puss and I got on famously, but he was obviously suffering from stress and the loss of his proper owner. This manifested itself in various ways, the worst of which was the bringing into the home of small "gifts" for me. Dead field mice would put in regular appearances in unexpected places, scaring the living daylights out of me. But by far the worst were the birds. If they were caught cleanly and despatched, then that would be that, but unfortunately Puss was either not a skilled despatcher, or he thought that it was great fun to get a bird into the dining room and enter into fun and games with it. Many were the times that I would walk in late in the evening to find a veritable bloodbath. On one famous occasion when I had been away for a couple of nights on business, I returned to find no curtains in the dining room at all. Carol told me the next morning that they were so badly bloodstained that she had taken them down and sent them off to the cleaners.

It felt so odd walking back into my cottage late at night, unable to draw those thick curtains across the dining room window, both to keep in the warmth and to keep out prying eyes. I still had in the back of my mind the occasion when we had been burgled, and I was reluctant to offer the slightest opportunity to be taken to the cleaners once again by a burglar, whilst at the same time being taken there by my wife!

To cap it all, I didn't realise, until my divorce came along, that my first wife was less enamoured of dogs than I. When she finally decamped, she was heard to say something, though not to me, to the effect of "thank God that I won't have to put up with all those hairs ever again. My life has been a nightmare for these last twenty-six years." I had absolutely no idea! She had concealed her aversion very well, and I was amazed that there were people in this world that didn't like dogs.

Why on earth didn't she say so years before?

These were difficult times, though, and I was grateful to Carol for keeping things running when I sunk into the slough of despond, and the demon alcohol ran my life for months on end.

Gradually, I licked my wounds and started to pick myself – and my business – up and start afresh.

It was twenty-five years or so since I had taken the reluctant step to become a professional hotelkeeper, and times had changed significantly. We were well and truly "on the map", and had all sorts of nationalities staying with us.

Japanese guests found it strange that there was no central hole in the bathroom floor to drain away water, but we could not be all things to all people, despite them always being ultra-polite.

Germans wanted their meals at strange times, mostly before the kitchen was properly open. For them, lunch was to be taken at noon on the dot, and they would be seen commandeering seats in the restaurant or on the terrace, perusing the menu from that moment on, wondering where their lunch was. At six o'clock their stomachs were informing them that it must be time for dinner. When told that dinner was never served before 7.30 p.m. they were often astounded. It was sometimes a hard conversion to English timings, not helped by my almost non-existent German and probably also because of the hour time difference to their homeland. Oh, and they liked big portions, too!

We had a lot of guests from the Netherlands. They too were unfailingly polite, perfectly charming, and spoke better English than most of the rest of the village. They also wrote nice thank you notes when they left, and left good tips for the staff, and that was much appreciated. Many of them descended upon us by motorbike. Clad in matching leathers which by themselves must have cost a small fortune, a couple would park an enormous BMW touring bike with large panniers on the car park. Their first question always was the same:

"Do you accept guests on motorbikes?" Then, after a brief hesitation, "Please?"

The first time that this happened, I was a bit doubtful, but seeing their ready smiles, and their bike, which I estimated cost much more than the car that I was running at that time, I said, "Yes, with pleasure!" Thereafter, when a big bike with Dutch plates rumbled up to the front door, I had no hesitation at all. Dutch people spent good money and never caused problems.

But by far the worst guests I encountered (and here I risk alienating people, but I am not maligning an entire country) were the French. Did they not have full sets of bed-linen in France, I sometimes wondered? Did they think that we might not notice when a sheet went missing from the bed – and always on the day of their departure?

They could be supercilious in their treatment of the staff, which was strange because in their own country, service is respected as an honourable profession. Alternatively, they would leave their bedrooms in the most disgusting state, necessitating a full clean every morning. They were also not above having a couple of undeclared children sleeping on the floor, as we found on many an occasion. I remember one morning being called up to a bedroom by a chambermaid.

"You just have to come upstairs and see the state of this room, sir."

"OK, give me a couple of minutes, and I'll be with you."

I trotted off upstairs to the offending room, to be greeted by an extremely large pile of McDonalds cartons and bags, some still containing the greasy and smelly remnants of their meal from the previous night. The stuff was strewn everywhere, and there were dirty marks on the bedlinen where they had wiped their fatty fingers. There was clear evidence of more than the allotted couple sleeping in the room and I wondered just how they had managed to sneak extra people in. Once I had got over the shock, I pondered where on earth all that McDonalds stuff had come from. There could not have been one of their outlets within at least twenty miles.

It forever remained a mystery – that and their French love of McDonalds over and above a restaurant with 2 AA Rosettes!

How we all hated the Health & Hygiene people. Yes, I realised that they had a job to do, and a very necessary one at that for some, but it was just another layer of ever-increasing officialdom, often pompous in approach, that we had to put up with.

All of the staff who handled food, myself included, had to qualify for the new Hygiene Certificate, and thereafter we had to display those certificates where they could easily be seen by the general public. I really didn't believe that my customers wanted to see a great long line of certificates for people whose names they might never know and who did jobs for which they might never be seen. How much more sensible, I thought, to have one certificate in a prominent position stating that the hotel had passed all of the relevant tests, even giving a score? But such was a few years away in the future...

Those H&H officials would descend on us, always without an appointment (sensible), often at the most inconvenient of times (not so sensible) to do their hygiene checks. These people would turn up at the desk unannounced and then proceed to put on white work coats and daft-looking white headgear complete with hairnet right there in the main hall. Anyone passing by could reasonably assume that they were with us to investigate an outbreak of bubonic plague.

Quite how was one to check fridge temperatures in the middle of a busy service, when the doors to those same fridges might be opened rather frequently? There were bound to be some temperature discrepancies.

They shuffled around in their uniforms, often without even the salutary "Good morning" to anyone. It must have taken a really special sort of person to have got the job.

"Any chance of you getting yourselves ready in a more appropriate place?" I would ask politely.

And on another occasion, "Would you mind terribly if I asked you to come into the hotel in future through the rear service door?"

The phrase "water off a duck's back" always came to mind. No, it was not their job to give undue consideration towards hotel guests, so, no, they would not. And it wasn't as though we were a high-risk business. All of our machinery, by this time, was literally state of the art and reliable. All of our commercial quality fridges had exterior controls and dials showing their inner core temperatures, as indeed did our new German walk-in cold room. In addition, we kept the regulation log books for recording daily temperatures, and the kitchens were cleaned according to a pre-approved schedule. Woe betide any chef that sloped off early on a quiet night and left the pot boy to clean up after them. That sort of problem would be the kiss of death. Everyone has seen examples of health and hygiene failures in their local newspapers. It must take a very long time to recover from that type of bad exposure, if indeed one ever could recover.

We were determined not to fall prey to that sort of offence, and we all worked very hard to maintain our high cleanliness rating. We improved on the official check list and got it approved for the next visit. There was only one occasion on which I panicked. Whilst the inspectors were doing their rounds, busy in the coffee shop, the kitchen and the restaurant, I hid myself away in my office with the log books in which regular temperatures had to be recorded. As I flicked through one of the relevant log books I found that it had not been completed for the last few days. A rush of panic engulfed me, and I came out in a cold sweat! Picking up a couple of different coloured biros for some semblance of authenticity, I filled in all of the missing entries, consumed by guilt. I had only just finished bringing it up to date when they descended on me. A narrow escape indeed – and a super-sized rocket for the head chef!

Quite why we had to have a problem with our dustbins, only a jobsworth at the council could explain. We managed for a number of years with regular-sized dustbins, which the bin-men would come and empty every week. As we developed, we bought more bins. It was a simple and straightforward service that suited everyone from time immemorial. And then came the new business rating system…

Once the local council woke up to the fact that they could extract more money from local businesses, they introduced ridiculous hikes to our business rates and we were thereafter made to pay extra for an allegedly improved service, though in fact it was exactly the same as before, just itemised separately on their invoice. Since my mother lived on the premises, she qualified for an exempt household bin, which was deemed private as it was technically allocated to my mother for her personal use only.

As things at the local council modernised, and the need for more money became ever more powerful an incentive, they told us that we would have to move the bins onto the roadside so that the hygiene refuse disposal operatives (bin-men to you and me) could more easily remove their contents. We simply could not do that and there was a bit of an impasse until they offered to provide one of those huge green bins for our waste, provided that it was parked out on the main road so that the lorry could pick up and empty it as it passed at about five o'clock in the morning. Oh, and there would be a hefty increase of charge for that! Such is deemed progress.

A nice idea to welcome guests as they arrived at an upmarket country house hotel – a large green bin, probably giving off fumes in high summer. And who was going to trundle it along to its newly designated space? Not I.

The remaining pub at the end of the village had taken to using a private collection service (also using similar big green bins, just with a different name on them) and they told me that it was excellent. I asked if they would mention it to the driver next time he came around. And so almost immediately a representative called on me and we not only fixed a price that massively undercut the council charge, but they were far more accommodating as to where the bin had to be sited, which, of course, was a huge benefit to all of us.

I took enormous pleasure in sending the local council off with a flea in their corporate ear. The very next day, a chap called in from said council and told me that they would cut their price in half (yes, in half!) if I would stay with them. Too late, was the cry! Within six months, every commercial premises in the village had moved away from the District Council, costing them a small fortune in lost revenue. I thought that it served them jolly well right, but I pondered the impact of that lost revenue throughout my village and beyond.

Meanwhile, I had taken in upon myself to be the winter gutter clearer. There seemed to be an inordinate number of gutters and downpipes around the hotel, and all rather too high up for my liking. Most were black cast iron, and the remainder black plastic, but all were in the least hospitable places to reach. I confess readily to a fear of heights, so standing on an orange box is enough to bring on a fit of the vapours.

When all the leaves had blown off the nearby trees, and the first overflowing gutter manifested itself by water cascading downwards instead of gurgling unseen through a pipe, I would be found lugging an ancient sent of ladders from the store, and propping them up against a wall so that I could reach a bit of flat roof halfway up the building.

Having reached that temporary security, I would vacillate, looking hither and thither, waiting until I had plucked up sufficient courage to make the next ascent. I suppose that it took me at least half a day of abject terror to achieve my goal, throwing sodden clumps of moss and compressed leaves – and more often than not a dead bird or two and a couple of wooden rods from spent firework rockets – over the parapet on to unsuspecting guests loitering below.

Why did I do it? Well, somebody had to, and I suppose it was pride that stupidly kept me doing it, year after year, when I could have been better occupied elsewhere. But, oh, the relief and sense of achievement as I returned my ladders to the storeroom, to languish untouched and unloved by myself until the approach of the next winter.

I can never look at a gutter nowadays without having to suppress a shudder.

We owned all of our linen, sheets, towels, tablecloths, serviettes and pillowcases when hotel life began for me, sending it off each week in dirty piles to a local laundry. Each item was marked with an identification mark to ensure that we got our own supply back. After a few years, and as business progressed, I learned that commercial laundries serving hotels were offering a linen hire option. I telephoned and asked someone to come and explain it all to me, which they did, although the explanation got rather lost on me and I was left baffled by the complexity of the switching arrangement. Thankfully, Carol got to grips with it better than I.

A couple more quotations later, between us we picked what appeared to be the least complicated of the three. A huge white van turned up, emblazoned on both sides with a gargantuan logo together with the name of the company and some slogan about hotel laundry services. I told the driver to park around the back.

What seemed to be a vast quantity of assorted linens were unloaded. It seemed to go on for ever and Carol came, puffing and panting, to inform me of our very first laundry problem.

"There's too much of it!"

"What do you mean, too much. You just sign for what was on the original order, surely?"

"I reckon that there is twice as much as we need!! Where's it all to go?"

I thought it best to go and have a word with the driver before I lambasted the company down the telephone. It was surely some simple mistake.

"Morning. Help us out here please. There seems to be an almost never-ending stream of linen being disgorged from your van."

The driver looked up to the sky, no doubt thinking what idiots we all were.

"Well, sir, you are not the first to ask. They should have told you."

"Told us what?"

"Well, the initial delivery is for two complete loads of everything on your order sheet, and here it all is." He waved his hand at the mountain of white stuff. "At the end of the first week, you bag up all that you have used, label it, and return it to us. You then start to use the quota for the second week, and so on. By that time, the third week, we will have returned your first lot of linens to you, freshly laundered. In that way, there are always three weeks' worth of linens within your and our system, so you will never run out, will you?"

I looked at Carol. She looked at me, and the penny dropped.

"Aha!"

I retired from that skirmish, leaving Carol to take on the reins for the future. She did it so well, that we eventually and unwittingly possessed sufficient linen of different shapes and sizes to stock a number of hotels. Indeed, we became the "go to" contact when other hotels in the vicinity ran short. At one stage a Best Western hotel pleaded with me for a huge pile of my stock because their own (from a different laundry) had not turned up and the weekend was upon them and they were fully booked with a wedding party. I was happy to oblige, but the ensuing logistical exercise was indeed a nightmare for me, recovering our used stock from them with our marks on by the time that our own collection day came around.

How had we done it though, amassing such an overstocking situation? Well, I never really knew, because I kept my nose out of it each week when the stock was totted up. I did look at Carol's figures in the log book, and they seemed to be correct to me. I can only put it down to inefficiency of the laundry company. In the year just before I sold the hotel, we had garnered so much that there was not a spare cupboard in the hotel that did not possess laundry piled into it. Every spare space in my cottage was overtaken by the stuff. At one stage it even crept up into the attic rooms before I drew the line and asked the company to send a big van around.

I did manage to keep quite a bit back in reserve, just

in case, and the laundry took all the rest of it away and never offered me any explanation. I think they were as flummoxed as I was.

I think that VAT (Value Added Tax) was introduced in 1973 as a method, of course, of raising more taxes, and making use of the likes of myself, a small business owner, to do the Revenue's work for them. Why should I – and every other employer – be expected to be legally required to become an unpaid tax collector for the government – and to bear the legal liability for getting every single figure correct? That really grated on me, but there was to be no escaping.

Like thousands of others, no doubt, I had the greatest of difficulty in getting to grips with the minutiae of the extraordinarily over-complicated requirements. Government issue booklets rained down on me through the post, all couched in language so verbose and technical that despite burning the midnight candle, I was not much further forward. Why on earth were some things taxable and others not? It was difficult to comprehend the rationale behind it all. It was almost as though the Inland Revenue had made it all as complicated as possible, the better to catch us out. Why should food consumed on the premises be chargeable to VAT, whilst that identical food, if consumed on a take-away basis and off the premises, be VAT free? Amazingly, we suddenly started to see a huge increase in take-away packed lunches!

Not long after it all started, I was unlucky enough to be selected at random for what was known as an "in-depth VAT inspection". With quaking boots, on the appointed day, which I had been dreading, I greeted the VAT inspector and put him to work in an unheated bedroom (we had a lot of those that winter) in which we had set up a table and chair for his use. I heaped the table with every single ledger that I could think of, leaving him to become (hopefully) thoroughly bamboozled by the complexity of it all.

After an hour or two had passed, and I was certain that he would be frozen to the marrow, I popped my head around the door. Could I offer a coffee without it being seen as a bribe? Nothing ventured, nothing gained…

"Yes please!"

"What about some hot soup later on?"

"Yes please!"

In view of the cold snap that winter, I was not surprised that both offers were accepted with alacrity. It was bitterly cold both inside and outside the hotel, and although there was no snow, there was a hard frost that seldom relented throughout the day. Our rudimentary plumbing and heating system just couldn't cope with the extended pressure of being run at the maximum day after day.

He sat there, poor chap (I almost felt sorry for him), wrapped around by his overcoat, and it was quickly apparent that he knew little more of the ins and outs of the process than did I. Once over that initial hurdle, we got on fine, and he stayed chatting until he had drunk a lot of hot coffee and I guess he felt that he could put a respectable number of hours down on to his timesheet. A clean bill of health! Whew!

A few years later we had another of those inspections, and I was found to have under-declared the huge sum of £93 between the last inspection and the current one. That time the inspection was a lot more thorough and it took more than a full working day for the inspector to reach his conclusion. I was happy to pay up and thought that a lot of money could have been saved just by their office asking for a cheque without sending anyone along.

My last direct dealing with the VAT man came in the year before I sold the hotel.

He wrote to say that he thought that I had made a mistake with my latest return. He felt that he should bring to my attention that my figures were some five figures adrift in his favour over and above the pattern of my usual payments. I had to agree that it did seem strange, and it was clearly an error on my part. With immediate effect I handed over responsibility for VAT returns to an outside professional company.

I blamed my divorce but it made me realise though that not all VAT men were inhuman.

Chapter 13

What a Performance!

A few years earlier, we had begun hiring out the conservatory for the new-fangled idea of conferences. There was money to be made from companies using the room to have pep talks or product demonstrations, or whatever. A number of local companies gave us their regular support, and, of course, it was easy to budget for their requirements and to produce what they wanted on time through the day. Companies paid well and never seemed to complain, which I found to be much in their favour.

For the rest, the question was: does one want to be operating a country house hotel as a holiday destination or as a business destination where people would come for conferences, staying overnight or not, as the case may be?

The business people would take up residence in the lounge talking far too loudly into mobile telephones the size of house bricks, and latterly with a laptop glued to their fingertips, and it just wasn't comfortable to have all that going on when a family or a couple wanted to relax.

The same went for conferences, especially when the delegates wanted to stay overnight. They would monopolise the bar area, be less than self-effacing in the restaurant, and the feedback that we received from both sides was unsatisfactory. Day conference delegates also took over the car park, making it difficult for our guests to park on their return from a day out.

We were just not big enough to offer the sort of separation required between holiday and business guests. Business guests had to go. It was an easy decision in the early days – they were just too demanding of time and space.

Once – just once – we were persuaded to do a wedding reception. We knew the family locally of the bride-to-be, and they pushed quite hard for us to do it. The actual event was no problem, the problem was the more raucous guests hanging on and making life difficult for those staying with us. When you have regular repeat business, stuff like that can tip people over the edge and they don't come back.

No, we had our niche, and we decided to stay within it.

Within that little niche, we latched on to a brand-new national tourist board autumn promotion that was set to take the hotel industry, and the country, by storm. I don't think that the board has ever done such a successful promotion since.

The smart booklet, trumpeted throughout the likes of the *Daily Mail*, was entitled "Let's Go!" and it was an immediate sell-out. As soon as I heard of it in the offing, I applied, qualified, and signed up, and the first issue showed that I was not alone. Most decent hotels had joined in and

I was worried that there would not be enough customers to go around. Silly me! Hotels reported booming business as people booked up for a stay of two or three nights, usually over a weekend, and crucially also in off-season. We got our fair share of that business and expanded it out the following year to offer special rates for mid-week as well. As with "Pets Welcome" we found our catchment area to be anywhere up to a two-hour drive away from us, meaning that we were in direct competition with hotels situated anywhere up to 100 miles away.

All this stuff was a bit new, because most hotels – other than those in big cities and internationally famous – drew their clientele from much more locally. The short break market was now here to stay, and we were determined to be part of it. Blue sky thinking was needed to get the mind around the fact that guests were quite happy to travel further than we had thought, to stay somewhere "different". We decided to be very "different"! We had to learn to "sell" ourselves in all sorts of new ways.

Much to my delight, that called for more competitive analysis. Off I would go whenever I could find a couple of spare days, inevitably mid-week. The extraordinary thing – but completely obvious in hindsight – was that you can learn so much about an hotel, even your own hotel, when you are staying for a couple of nights; so much more than going for just dinner or afternoon tea. I would also recommend to any hotelier to spend a night in every one of their bedrooms. It is really surprising just what you will discover, and then be able to put right just for coppers, thus ensuring more repeat business.

A while later, a conference event was scheduled to take place in the south Lake District, and I wanted to go because there was something on the agenda that I thought could be of benefit. Though it was far away, it came at a time when I was happier to take a few days away, and it had the bonus of coming when I had recently met the stunning lady who was to become my second wife.

We travelled together to the venue, chatting animatedly and enjoying each other's company. Sally is a Lancashire lass, and "sand grown" as the locals are wont to say of anyone born within sight of Blackpool Tower, which means about half of Lancashire since the Fylde coast is so flat. The youngest of three children, her parents were retired and she held a very senior position in a well-known international group. Towering over me when in her heels, slender and always immaculately turned out, she was not known to suffer fools gladly. I determined to remain on my best behaviour – well, for a while anyway.

Sally had an interest in the forthcoming proceedings too, so it was doubly worthwhile to make the effort to go there. After much winding down country roads with grey clouds scudding overhead and threatening rain, we arrived at the hotel complex which was to be our base. The hotel hosting the event was a traditionally-built Lakeland dwelling with lots of dark slate, dreary stone walls, the whole giving a dour and gloomy effect. It could only be better inside, surely? We had booked in for three nights, with the tourism meeting lasting over two days. The rain began in earnest as we rushed from the car to the front door, the downpour catching us neatly with large splashes. It was to rain from our arrival to our departure, as so often it does in that area of the country, I had been told.

The first day of meetings was interesting, and I made some valuable notes which I thought I could apply to my own circumstances. My concentration wavered occasionally, though, because I could see large trickles of water coming through the ceiling and turning patches of the carpet into a soggy swamp. Management was called, and in they came with a whole battalion of buckets at the ready. It must have been a regular problem for them, to possess so many buckets. The meeting was cut short and broke up in some chaos as everyone took advantage of the free tea and coffee offered by the hotel as some compensation. Later on, dinner was the usual turgid affair of standard conference fare eaten at large round tables for ten persons, all delegates looking glumly around themselves wondering what to talk about to persons that they did not know. The rain, both inside and outside, had really put a dampener on proceedings.

There was little enthusiasm for the bar afterwards and we all retired for the night. However, breakfast was something else again. We all came down to breakfast as arranged, far too early for my liking, to find the conference room still shrouded in darkness; there were no water glasses, no notepads, nothing for the day had been prepared. Even worse, and of more immediacy, the dining room was also in darkness, with the curtains to the downstairs rooms still firmly closed. Upon investigation, the kitchen was shut, too, and similarly unlit. Nobody was to be seen other than us early delegates.

Could we raise anyone? No, we could not, though we tried hard, ringing bells and calling out loudly. What was to be done? The place was just like the Marie Celeste, and presumably the management had forgotten to give instruction – or perhaps the staff had all walked out? Who was to know?

"You up for this?" A colleague waved to catch my attention from across the room.

I nodded back. What was I letting myself in for?

"Anyone else?"

"Yes."

"Count me in too."

And so, four intrepid hoteliers in our group, used to taking command of unforeseen circumstances, walked into the kitchen, got our bearings, lit up the burners and got to work. We produced about fifteen cooked breakfasts complete with tea, coffee and toast by the time that the first staff member put in an appearance. He was just nonplussed and stared at us, cowering in a corner like a rabbit in the headlights. Others trickled in, gaped in shocked surprise, and eventually some semblance of business as usual commenced. None of them, however, complained at our initiative.

Over an hour late, we began the conference again. We then sat with the buckets and the continuous drip… drip… drip through the morning meeting. There were a lot of galvanized buckets and those drips were magnified sufficiently to make proceedings nigh on impossible.

And then, of course, it could only get worse. The manager called the organisers to one side for a private conversation during elevenses. I briefly wondered if he had spotted me in his kitchen and was about to complain, but no, it was not that.

"I know that you have a reservation for another night," he said. "Well, I am sorry, but I am going to have to ask you to leave by the end of the day."

"Eh? What on earth have we done?"

"No, no, it's not you. The whole hotel has been booked for tonight by the local Young Farmers Association for their entire North of England Annual Conference, and there are no spare bedrooms. We must have overbooked you. Sorry about that."

"You are joking, surely?"

"Sadly, no."

We could have argued, of course, on the basis that not only had we booked, but we were in possession already of all the rooms. Frankly, we were happy to beat a retreat from the place and go and find somewhere dry. We moved south towards Blackpool for the night, the conference being effectively a write-off from that lunchtime. A very few years later, I happened to hear that the hotel had shut up shop and had been turned into a caravan and mobile home site. Good luck to them; they probably never got the roof fixed.

I had never heard of the PRS (Performing Rights Society) whose main reason for existence appeared to be to try to conjure extra funds for their members from the likes of us poor unsuspecting hoteliers, so it came as a bit of a shock when I first received their unsolicited invoice in the post. It went straight into the nearest bin.

They had cottoned on to the fact that, as we modernised and upgraded to meet increasing guest expectations, hotels such as mine were installing a TV (albeit pretty small and basic) in each bedroom. Basically, they wanted money every time anyone switched on a television or played recorded music.

Before the arrival of the modern age of satellite TV in every hotel bedroom, we had installed a TV set into a ground floor lounge that we adventurously entitled according to a sign on the door "Television Room". It was right next to the main lounge, and many years later the two rooms would be knocked into one, using a graceful archway and a wide polished oak threshold to bridge the thickness of the interior wall.

I can't remember now what we paid for that TV, and I suppose that there was a licence requirement even in those days. But those beggars at the PRS wrote to me asking how many televisions there were in the hotel. I declined to answer their letter and declined also to provide them with the information that they sought in a series of letters couched in ever more aggressive terms. Eventually, some poor chap hove over the front portal – without appointment – and demanded to see me. He told me who he was, and I told him that I was sorry, but I was out. He blinked first and departed.

He returned another day, by appointment, and, to his credit, not by a raise of an eyebrow did he admit that we had met before. He told me that his head office was quartering the country to tell hotels that once there had been TV installed in every bedroom, PRS would want a licence fee paid for each bedroom TV and that they were entitled by law to receive it. Oh, and whilst they were at it, they wanted another separate fee for any background music played in public areas of the hotel, chargeable as well. And they wanted it all every year henceforth!

What bugged me was the illogicality of their position. Firstly, not every bedroom in an hotel, and certainly mine, was occupied every night. Secondly, who was to say that an occupant would even turn on their TV? And thirdly, let's say that there were ten guests one evening: why should they pay ten times more than when they were sitting in our TV room all together? All in all, I thought, it was just too barmy.

I could see another court case looming on the horizon. So, back I went to our main trade organisation, the BHRCA, (the British Hotels Restaurants and Caterers Association, to give it its overlong mouthful of a title), that told me off the record that they agreed with me, but that publicly, they must stand four-square with the new law and support the PRS.

I wrote to the PRS, returning their invoices, and invited them to take me to court, stating that I was happy to provide myself and my business as a test case on behalf of the rest of the membership. I copied it to the BHRCA and everywhere else that I could think of that might be interested, including the local newspaper. I received a letter back from the PRS, stating that they acknowledged receipt of my solitary licence fee but that I still owed for the balance. The same thing happened each year thereafter, and the arrears continued to mount. I wrote to them refusing to pay, they acknowledged receipt of my single licence, and they never took me to court.

This position lasted right up until I sold the business on retirement, many years later. In hindsight, I think that I may just have forgotten to mention that problem to the incoming purchasers.

I could foresee a time when further and further impositions would be heaped on hotel businesses, forcing them either to close down through extra operating costs and/or moving them into strategic alliances with, for example, marketing consortiums. It was time to get on board with others in order to have greater clout in circumstances such as this. The BHRCA had proved, as usual, to be a toothless watchdog.

I had by then attended quite a few meetings of the local tourist board, wanting to see what was going on elsewhere and what developments might be coming. It turned out to be a forum for a few people to talk their hind legs off about whatever was bugging them at the time. A lack of control meant that there were just chattering forums where no seeming advantage was to be gained.

And so instead, I turned my focus in a different direction and expressed interest in a new type of independent hotel consortium, still in its infancy, to be run by its members, for its members. A new board of directors was to be appointed, and I was asked to put my name forward. Nothing ventured, nothing gained, I thought, so I jumped in feet first and sat around an inaugural board meeting with half a dozen other hoteliers whom I had never met before that first get-together. Roles were handed out, and to my consternation I was landed with the position of Administration Director, something that I knew next to nothing about other than in the context of my own small business.

An office was duly rented and a lovely matronly middle-aged lady by the name of Joyce was hired as its sole occupant – for the time being anyway. I was supposed to pop in regularly to sort out any problems and co-ordinate mailshots and the like in an effort to attract more members. I quickly learned that Joyce knew a heck of a lot more about what was required than I did, and I quietly left her to get on with it. I enjoyed driving over there through the lush green countryside to take afternoon tea and biscuits with her, and that was my main input, other than helping to stuff and seal envelopes for the frequent mailshots to seek to increase the membership.

We got on rather well, did Joyce and I, but the axe was to fall on her within the year. Other directors reasoned with a complete lack of logic that an office in a pleasant market town less than an hour from London, with a direct rail link from a London main line station, was totally inconvenient and the office was moved forthwith to Wales – work that one out if you can. My role was over in that particular portfolio. It was a major slap in the teeth, but I felt that I should continue to hang in there. I did feel guilty about poor Joyce though for a long time. It was a salutary lesson on how (not) to treat staff.

As a speaker of French, I then had another unpaid job foisted upon me, one which I enjoyed and which was to develop nicely over the years, and take me to a number of European capital cities, and more besides, as we forged links with like-minded consortia in a dozen countries. I spent quite some time at the head office in Switzerland and that itself gave me an extra insight into hotelkeeping. There were terribly long-winded meetings at that Swiss Head

Office, where future policy and pricing were thrashed out in order to try to bring together such a disparate group of privately or family-owned hotels in a number of European countries. Then the dreaded internet first raised its head, and like some electronic octopus, sought to weave its tentacles into every tiny corner of the operation. I confessed to knowing nothing about computers, booking systems on-line, and other such wizardry. I felt that I should sit in a far corner of the meeting room with a dunce's hat on.

It was to be a hard learning curve for me, and although I made progress, I always felt that I lagged behind in that area. My talents, modest as they were, lay in other directions.

Not all meetings were held in the Swiss Head Office. Once a year there was a huge jamboree of an event to which all member hotels were invited. I still remember the one that was held in Biarritz where I was invited, at literally five minutes' notice, to give an extended speech in French to the delegates, explaining the progress of the British contingent. I seemed to have got away with it and sat down, trembling all over, to enthusiastic applause and back slapping. But the cat was out of the bag, and I could never henceforth get away with pretending not to understand all the conversations and asides at the meetings which I was probably never meant to understand anyway.

Another interesting annual event that Sally and I attended was in Sicily.

it was part of my duties for the consortium and the European contingent had made that choice for the venue. So, at least I got my own ticket paid. After the conference was over, this gave us the chance to relocate to a lovely old villa type hotel, right on the beach, almost within sight of Taormina, and over which brooded the towering presence of Mount Etna. I was secretly hoping for a bit of an eruption whilst we were there. But our surprise came in a different form altogether, that of an upmarket Italian wedding reception.

The Hotel Villa Sant' Andrea overlooked the sea, almost had its feet in the water, and indeed it featured its own private beach and landing stage. We lazed on that beach on our first day, doing very little. Dinner that evening was just perfect, taken by candlelight, and featuring the most exquisite food, washed down by a local wine. I always think it odd that local wine tastes wonderful when in the right setting, but is just like vinegar when taken home as a gift for friends. The next day we spent exploring Taormina, a beautiful and historic town. The morrow was earmarked for the trip up the volcano.

Walking back into our hotel, we noticed that there was some sort of function in full swing in the hotel, with a gathering of people done up to the nines; the ladies turned out as only stylish Italians can do. We made our way to the bar, where the barman, the same one as the previous night, nodded to us and handed over two flutes of rather good champagne.

"No, sorry, there has to be some mistake! We wanted two Campari and sodas."

With a broad smile, he replied, "It's on the house tonight. It's a particularly good champagne for these people, so enjoy it!"

"But, but…"

And with that we downed our champagne. Very soon, two further glasses were placed before us. The barman nodded, and so we drank anew.

Neither of us can remember exactly how many times this procedure was repeated, but we soon found ourselves in the midst of a cluster of those Italians who, I have to assume, thought that we were eccentric English cousins who had just flown in. My Italian is only so-so, but Sally can be very gregarious. We were plied anew with champagne, and just before we virtually passed out, we managed to extricate ourselves from our new friends to weave our way back to our bedroom, which thankfully was on the ground floor. Dinner was completely forgotten.

And the trip to the top of the volcano, scheduled for the next morning? We cried off, or to be more truthful, slept right through it instead. What a night to remember, most of which we have unfortunately forgotten!

When I had first introduced a rota board for staff working over the Christmas and New Year periods, it caused uproar.

"Sir, I never realised that I would have to work then. We always have a family do. I'll be expected."

"Well," said I, "you can still go to part of it, can't you?"

"Dunno." With a sullen shrug of the shoulders.

"Let me put it this way. The hotel is open then, likely to be full, and takes more money over that period than in either of the two months on either side. Working whilst we stay open over Christmas and New Year helps me to be able to keep you on and pay you during quieter periods. If you want to work here, you have to work when the hotel is busy. Surely you can see that?"

This would be greeted with another shrug and, if I was lucky "Oh, well. I suppose so."

What really infuriated me was when someone called in "sick" just before Christmas, to avoid their rota, placing extra burdens on those that did turn up. But they only did it once…

One year my mother asked me, out of the blue, if we could close the hotel for Christmas, saying:

"Wouldn't it be lovely if we could just have a family Christmas and sit by the fire, doing nothing much at all? It must be a huge effort for you, putting on the great show over Christmas and the New Year. And Sally would like it, I'm sure…"

I couldn't deny that her words held a certain resonance. Besides, I had been thinking about closing for a few days over the coming Christmas. My reasons were slightly different, though. Putting on a full-blown Christmas in a country hotel is necessarily an expensive affair.

The clientele that comes for five days for a country house Christmas party expect the world. OK, they do pay for that, but the effort to produce a show for them, day after day, is truly immense. Factor in that staff costs are at least double, that some of them go AWOL at the last moment and everything that you buy to keep things running is also vastly more expensive. Last but definitely not least, there is that well-known Murphy's Law which states that "If it can break at Christmas, when all repairers are unavailable and away, then it will."

I almost lost count of the times that a boiler would expire or a major item of kitchen equipment would go on the blink. I learned to keep spare immersion rods in stock for the boilers, but I didn't possess the skills to repair them myself. Nor could I get a large commercial oven back to work when, for one reason or another, it had died. Electricity and I are simply not compatible. I can't see it...!

Two key staff became the catalyst for our Christmas closure that year. Both, months before had signed up to work over the Christmas and New Year period. But then, lo and behold, their families offered an irresistible alternative, probably with a three-line whip. I did the maths and worked it against the effort and found it very easy to give way and agree to my mother's suggestion of closing for Christmas.

A few days before, all our guests departed for their own Christmas festivities; there were few remaining decorations to be seen, parts of the hotel had been shut down with the heating left on the minimum setting, and goodbyes had been said to staff, with my fingers crossed that they would all turn up again in good time, a week later, for the planned New Year festivities.

We decided that it was all too much effort to keep the big oven and other kitchen kit fired up, so we repaired back to my cottage with my mother in tow. And there we had a very nice relaxing time for a few days. How strange it all was, when the actual day dawned. It seemed almost alien to lie in bed instead of dragging myself towards the bathroom in a rush to get over the road. Breakfast was a leisurely affair, conducted in dressing gowns and accompanied by the newspapers that I had held back. We managed to cobble a fine Christmas Day lunch together, with Sally masterminding the preparation and roasting of a goose, a novelty for me.

Not to be outdone, my mother wanted to do her bit towards the event. I recalled from my childhood that she was a dab hand at game chips and brandy butter too, though strangely I have absolutely no memories at all of her ever cooking a complete meal. Where on earth did they all come from? Anyway, her contribution was a great success, even if the kitchen in my cottage later resembled a disaster zone.

During the afternoon, my mother reminisced about all of those geese of yesteryear and how the old and mostly now long-forgotten droveways were used to get them to market at the Goose Fair in Nottingham. Some flocks (at least a hundred at a time) had been driven many miles and were a lot thinner than when they had started their journey. As a child, she had been taken out to see the spectacle.

Meanwhile, for my part, I recalled the tale of how one morning, on the way to the new kitchen, and walking through what remained of the old original hotel kitchen, I thought that I had been transported into another lifetime, a cross between Dante's Inferno and a Victorian Christmas. I had stopped dead in my tracks.

There at the far end of the room was an unrecognisable person covered almost entirely in feathers. Any feathers not attached to that person were swilling around the room like a cloud, all but obscuring the far doorway, before landing softly to form a light covering on the floor tiles, much as I imagine the interior of a duvet to be.

On closer inspection, the mystery person turned out to be my mother! What had got into her mind I do not know, but she had, unbeknownst to anyone else, decided that her contribution to that particular Christmas was going to be the plucking of all of the pheasants that had just been delivered. Swooping on the box of birds and snatching them away from the hapless potboy, she manoeuvred herself into a spare space, which happened to be adjacent to the top of a chest freezer. Clearly, tidiness was not going to be her watchword during this process. Feathers were pulled out, legs and heads were chopped off with gay abandon, and finally, the right hand was plunged into the bloody interior, emerging clutching a large handful of intestines, slimy heaps of which adorned the top of the freezer. Cleaning up after her was a bit of a trial, but I was glad that she had made the effort. I suppose that she could identify that with long bygone times and tasks that she had undertaken all those years ago.

Later in the day, we took the dogs for a walk to shake off the torpor of the heavy meal. Mother slept the afternoon away until it was time for her sherry and a light dinner. The itchy feet returned after Boxing Day and it was time to get back into gear to ready ourselves for the New Year party.

All too soon, I found myself slinking around the quiet and closed-up hotel premises, not really able to get my head around it all. Stock had to be ordered, fires prepared, staff rotas to be checked and reconfirmed, and heating had to be cranked back into action as it took a day or two to get the place warm in winter-time. While it had been great to have nothing to do for those few days, it really had put a dent into the winter period profits, and, lo and behold, we opened for the entire festivities the following year, and indeed every one thereafter.

Chapter 14

Disgruntled Guests

Weekends are times that we should all look forward to – whether as hoteliers welcoming new or returning guests, or as guests looking forward to a relaxing two or three days away, being pampered. It did not always work out quite as planned. But things seldom do…

I am pleased to say that by that time we were virtually always fully booked at weekends, particularly so in mid-winter when we ran a range of special offers to drum up business. Special discounted offers were frowned upon until quite recently by a certain section of the industry. However, the name of the game, in my book, was to fill as many rooms as possible, provided that I could see an overall profit. Repeat business was always best, because it generated extra income for no extra outlay. Business from "Pets Welcome" and "Let's Go" was also gratefully received, a happy marriage on both sides.

But there were the inevitable exceptions, when guests came with misconceptions of what to expect. No matter how truthful your advertisement might be, there is always someone who will have read it the wrong way. For example, the couple with two teenage children who stood in the hall asking, "Where's the skittle alley, then?"

"I believe that the nearest one is in the county town, some twenty miles distant, sir!"

From where did they get the notion that we possessed a skittle alley in the first place? That was one of the daftest queries lobbed at us over the reception desk – and believe me, there were a lot.

The most recent curmudgeon to have crossed over the hotel threshold was late in the afternoon, and it being a Friday, it was, as usual, raining cats and dogs. Wet Fridays are never a good thing in my experience in the hotel business. Gravel flew as a large antiquated Daimler crunched up to the front door and skidded to a halt outside, leaving a couple of unsightly gouges in the gravel that has been so painstakingly raked that morning. The driver pushed hard on his horn. In reception, Carol and I looked at each other and wondered what was going on. Then, another blowing of the horn, followed a minute later by an exasperated overweight middle-aged gentleman bursting through the door, trailing gusts of wind and scattering raindrops in his wake.

And no, he did not consider it to be a politeness to close the door.

"I hooted! Twice! Could you not hear me? Where's the ruddy car park?" He bellowed, shaking the rain off his pork pie hat, his moustache all aquiver with belligerence.

The customary greetings of "hello" or "good evening" had clearly passed him by. He ran his hand through his thinning hair, sweeping a scanty comb-over back into position, and glared at us. Carol stood by the desk, smoothing down her uniform along the lines of her trim figure; it usually had the desired effect when levelled at irascible guests. Before she could say anything though, I gritted my teeth and walked back to the yawning open front door, asking the newcomer to follow me. I peered out into the rain and I could see that his wife was huddled down in the passenger seat, timid as a church mouse; quite clearly, she would have liked to have been anywhere else at that particular moment. Clearly also, she was used to the bombastic utterances of her husband that would surely wreck their weekend before it had even properly started.

After giving both of them my usual courteous and warm greeting (which I have found usually has the calming effect of turning away most wrath) I pointed to the clearly visible car park to the side of the hotel, and to the large cream-and-forest-green sign on which were writ large the magic words "To The Hotel Car Park – Private. For the Use Of Hotel Guests Only", illuminated both by discreet lighting below it, and more glaringly by his own headlights.

No, as you may guess, no word of either apology or thanks was forthcoming.

A couple of minutes later, in he barrelled, followed a couple of paces behind by his more self-effacing wife, both of them shaking more water all over the place as they removed their topcoats, and leaving the door wide open once more. A handy gale was building up in the hall, threatening to extinguish the log fire, and pushing wisps of grey smoke all over everywhere. The timid lady cowered back as though she knew what was going to happen next.

"We would have been here hours ago if it was not for the wife being a complete nincompoop when it comes to reading a map. How does anyone expect to be able to get it right when you hold it upside down? I've lost count of the times that I've told her about that." And with that, he threw another baleful glare back at his long-suffering spouse.

So, the man was clearly a bully.

Our studied professionalism wavered not a millimetre, and the offer of a hot pot of tea, or something stronger, was instantly made by Carol, who made a quick dash for the nether regions of the hotel to set the wheels in motion.

"No! We'll have the tea as soon as we come down, a bit later on." He said this without bothering to turn and consult his wife. And with that, they made for the stairs, his wife lugging the larger of their two cases. Now, in any decent hotel – and we were by then a very decent hotel, in my opinion – two things always happen at this stage. The first is that it is the custom, even enshrined in law, for guests to sign in, in some format, upon arrival. The second is that we offer to carry bags and show people to their rooms. We make no exceptions.

"Aha, excuse me, sir! Sir? Sir! Please just come back here to the desk and sign in."

"No, no, I can't be bothered with all that sort of nonsense. We wrote, so you know who we are." This said from about three steps up our staircase.

"No, I don't," I mumbled quietly to myself. "Well, sir, in that case there is not much point in you both going further up the staircase because you won't know where your room is, nor be able to gain access to it. Will you, sir?"

Bags were banged down and the disgruntled punter came back to the desk.

No, it was just not going to be a nice weekend, this one, if the first guests to arrive were all going to be like this. I was already beginning to think about whether to ask them to leave, when I caught the eye of the timid mouse-wife who was looking pleadingly at me. I thought better of it and gave her a slight nod and a smile.

And that reminds me of another set of weekend guests a year or two later, though the weather was kinder that weekend. An almost new Bentley Continental, rather garishly painted in a bright metallic kingfisher blue sat in the car park one afternoon, straddling the white lines and taking up two spaces. I could just see through the darkened windows that the interior was finished in white leather with blue piping. More suitable for Los Angeles than the leafy lanes of rural England, I thought, with a slight sniff before I caught myself. One of my dogs then proceeded to relieve itself against the front wheel before I could stop it. "Huh", I thought, "that dog is thinking just what I'm thinking." And with that, I started my duties in the hotel for the evening, thinking no more about it.

Much later, in the bar and lounge, the evening menus were being distributed, drinks and orders being taken. By the time that most guests had departed towards the restaurant, there remained just one couple, the oddest couple that you ever did see. Both looked as though they had just been dragged through a hedge backwards, and were clad in what looked to me like Oxfam rejects. His hair was a tangled and unkempt mess and his jeans had rips and holes in them, through which extensive views of scrawny white knees were clearly to be seen. A tatty leather aviator jacket over a white t-shirt covered the rest of him. His accompanying lady was dressed little better, although I could not help but notice the length of her coltish legs stretching out from the shortest of leather mini-skirts. She would have been truly beautiful even without the heavy layer of make-up and the rim of kohl around her eyes. The sharp cut of her hair must have cost a fortune.

Younger staff members were agog. Whispering and nudging each other, I finally caught on.

"Well, go on, tell me… Who is it then?"

They were keen to point the man out as an internationally known rock and roll star who had recently ended a world tour on a high in London. I nodded politely and passed on by, trying very hard not to eye the lady's legs.

He and I came face to face the very next morning right after breakfast. I had been told that he had been difficult all through dinner the previous evening, making himself and his fame known to all and sundry, complaining particularly at the length of time it had taken to provide their cooked-to-order à *la carte* meals.

Now, the problem had been his breakfast egg. "I burned my mouth on it," he said, whining just like a petulant child. I was quite nonplussed for a moment until I realised that he was serious. I think I did offer an apology, and then I wondered why I had done so.

"I'm so sorry, sir, about hot eggs reaching your table for breakfast. But are not eggs for breakfast almost, by definition, hot? And, permit me to say, but you are surely old enough to know that fact without the need to be coddled?" The pun was not intended, and I am sure that it passed over him anyway. A wry smile fleetingly appeared on his young lady's face, as she caught on.

I heard a couple of quiet laughs in the background from other guests. It had not been my intention to humiliate the chap, but, rather than just taking it on the chin, he then went into a lengthy diatribe about the hotel, the service, the fact that they had been woken overly early by the sound of birdsong – how strange to hear that out in the countryside! – and finally the absolute disaster of the hot eggs, that I somewhat abruptly cut him short.

"Sir, if you would care to go to your room and pack your belongings, I will have your account ready for you when you come back downstairs."

A moment of shocked silence was followed by the inevitable "Don't you know who I am?" followed by, "But we are booked in for another night here!"

"No, actually, I don't know who you are. But you created such a fuss last evening, and then again this morning, that I really think that you don't fit in here at all, and that you will be happier elsewhere." The childish tantrum that ensued was enough for a couple of guests to lean over and congratulate me on maintaining our standards. All that over boiled eggs!

One of the guests summed it all up admirably: "That chappie has probably not washed for weeks. Not suitable at all."

All hotels receive complaints: some are justified, but many are not. I suppose that we got our fair share over the years, perhaps more than the average because I was, after all, operating a fairly idiosyncratic business which flew in the face of what many might see as the standard model.

Although I had briefly attended catering college all those years ago, I had received no formal training in the operation of an hotel, although for my particular circumstances, it probably did not matter too much. We learned everything on the hoof, amending and improving as we went along and I always had a clear vision of where I wanted to get the business to sit in my chosen market. All very well, provided that I got things right, and that I was favoured by a liberal dusting of that magic ingredient – luck.

Some of the complainers who stayed at our hotel were people who would seemingly enjoy themselves, pay up without a murmur and depart with a cheery wave and a promise to see us next year, then a few days later a letter would arrive from them stating some sort of grievance and asking for some, or all, of their money back. It is a peculiarly British trait, I have decided, not to complain at the time if you have a grievance. For a hotelier, it makes it simply impossible to identify afterwards the cause of the incident and to sort things out to everyone's satisfaction. I think that over some 35 years I could count on one hand the times that we felt the need to offer a refund. When we did so, we did it with good grace and learned from our mistake.

We did have a serious complaint to consider one morning, however. We had started to do business with a rather upmarket tour operator in Scotland, who would send bespoke clients on trips by car, using us as one of the stopovers – or destinations as they were known – on a motoring holiday. The itinerary usually provided for three or four days with us. One such couple had been staying for three days, and were occupying one of our nicest rooms, one of the new garden rooms.

On the fourth morning, the day of their departure, the husband and wife presented themselves at reception, she with a bandage over her upper arm. In some distress, she said that she had burned her arm on the heated towel rail when she got up in the night and had to use the en-suite bathroom. She now wished to complain, stating that the towel rail was far too hot for the intended purpose, and was therefore dangerous.

This was a new one to me, and I was most concerned.

"I am so sorry! Could I see the injury, please? Shall I get a doctor?" I was horrified.

"No! No doctor!" She looked alarmed at the thought. I wondered why she was so vehement. "I'll visit my own when we get home."

She then peeled off part of the bandage and thrust her arm over the counter for me to look at. Indeed, she did have a burn mark on her arm. Not being a doctor, I could not tell when it had occurred.

"We will be suing you when we get back to Scotland!" she said, adding that places like ourselves should check our electrical equipment to see that things like this should never happen.

After so long in the business, you develop a nose, a sixth sense, when people are stringing you along. I had no proof, but I was doubtful. As she had said that she would sue us, I thought it prudent to keep my counsel and limit myself to profuse apologies, without admitting any liability.

A number of us trooped into the bedroom and checked the temperature of the towel rail. It seemed OK, but I made a mental note for Carol to call out our friendly local electrician to give it the once-over.

And so, they packed their bags and departed, and in due course a letter arrived, not from their lawyer, but from the tour operator, detailing the facts as they had been given to them, and already judging us to have been at fault. Unless they received a satisfactory explanation and agreement to a complete refund for that client, they proposed to withdraw my hotel from their brochure and send no more customers to us, citing the danger and hazard to the public.

There was something niggling at the back of my mind over her burn. It had not seemed that much inflamed, and I was sure that it would have been, to have caused such a mark. And there was something else, but I couldn't pin it down. I called over one of the female members of staff and asked her to accompany me to the bedroom in question.

Carol, at reception, raised a quizzical eyebrow. I ignored her and the two of us went to the room, which was in the process of being cleaned and made up. I drew the thick curtains to darken the room.

"Right, Karen, go and lie down on the bed. Then pretend that you need to go to the loo and that it is the middle of the night. You have been in this room for the last three nights, so you don't need to switch the bedroom light on for fear of waking your husband. Go in to the loo, pretend to do what you need to do, and report back.

Off she went, calling through the closed door, "Do I turn on this light in here or not?"

"Good question! Do it twice, once with and once without. Check to see if there is a difference in your movements."

Well, to cut a long story short, there was no way that our dear departed guest could have burned her arm on that heated towel rail unless she had been a professional contortionist. Karen was unable to replicate the angle of the burn on her own arm, without twisting herself around into a completely unnatural position which, even half asleep in the middle of the night, she would have been totally unlikely to have done. So, I took photographs of the bathroom, the location of the towel rail vis-a-vis the loo, Karen trying to put her arm into the required position, and sent them up to Scotland, together with a note from our electrician to say that the towel rail checked out perfectly for output and was not overheating.

The case was closed immediately, but the damage was done, and we received no further guests from that tour operator.

But very occasionally, there does need to be a parting of the ways between guest and hotelier. Usually this happens when a guest is disgruntled about something, some perceived slight, whether real or imagined, they pack their bags and appear at the reception desk, demanding a substantially reduced bill. Then begins a series of questions, followed by a negotiation, ending up with either a discount being offered or an even more disgruntled customer when it is refused.

On the whole, I was a bit soft in these circumstances. The last thing that one needs is a stand-up verbal fisticuffs at check-out. It upsets other guests to hear annoyed, bellicose guests when you are fostering a loose type of house party atmosphere; and, it has to be said, it might give them ideas. You can well do without such people.

One such couple arrived over our threshold one (wet, of course) weekend evening. They had undergone the classic scenario of getting lost, getting wet, and fearing that they would be too late to bag the best room, or even missing dinner. To boot, they were by now not even talking to each other, the one blaming the other for everything going wrong. And, yes, it was all going to be our fault!

They shouted, they harangued each other, and they demanded this and that. Nothing that I said would please them by then; not even the offer of a free upgrade. It is very difficult to keep calm in these circumstances because stuff like this is exactly what you don't need at the start of a busy weekend. It upsets the rest of the guests and does my heart rate no good either. So, keeping my cool, I said:

"I have listened to everything that you have said, sir, or rather which you have shouted at me. It is quite obvious that nothing that we can do is going to make you happy here. Am I right?"

"Well, err, I…"

"So, please go! Just go!"

"What on earth do you mean? But…but…you can't do that!"

"I am afraid that I can, sir."

"Ah, but I've paid a deposit. I have my rights!"

"Carol!" Leaning back over my shoulder, I said, "Cheque book, please."

The man stood there absolutely fuming. I thought that his wife even had the glimmer of a smile on her face at his comeuppance.

I quickly wrote him out a cheque for his deposit, smacked it down on the counter, and sent him on his way. I wonder why I never heard again from him or his poor long-suffering wife? I probably only ever told anyone to leave half a dozen times in 35 years, though. Mostly it was because of unacceptable behaviour, particularly of the sexual shenanigans type, but the above was certainly the quickest. I came to learn over the years that the customer is definitely not always right, and just occasionally, I found it impossible to turn the other cheek.

One of my more savvy guests, a regular visitor a number of times each year, reckoned that my hotel ran a bit like a Swiss watch; smoothly and with everything in order and on time. A very nice comment, and one which was greatly appreciated by everyone on the staff, myself included. I, for my part, was particularly appreciative because he was another hotelier, owning a prosperous inn in deepest Devon. Clearly, he only caught us at the good times!

What makes a good hotel is often that which is taking place behind the scenes; like the proverbial swan gliding on the lake, all serene above, but with the legs of every single member of staff paddling like the clappers below. All most satisfactory provided the legs never go on show.

I often spent the early part of one evening moving about, occasionally chatting to a party in the bar, and then with some couples taking a pre-prandial tincture in the lounge. One such was a regular couple, and I will promote him and call him the Major. Tonight, he was with his wife and unmarried daughter, as she too lived locally, and we were one of his preferred ports of call. As I swept by, I just caught the tail end of his order:

"…and I'll have the prime fillet steak. Plain. Well done."

My step never faltered, although the pretty young waitress shot an imploring glance my way. No problem, I thought, just more of the same, and we have lived through worse and triumphed here before.

The schooners of sweet sherry duly imbibed, they were shown into the restaurant and took their seats. We had, of course, ensured that as regulars they had a good table, looking out over our gardens towards the valley, and then beyond to a line of low hills. In the valley, water glittered off the river in the remaining evening light, a shimmering silver thread in the gloaming, winding along into the far distance. Picture perfect, I thought.

Once seated, linen napkins were whisked from their places and deposited in laps. Warm bread, home-made of course (tonight it was tomato and olive) and butter were swiftly to hand. Soon, his preferred choice of prawn cocktail was put before him. No matter that it hadn't appeared on the menu since the '60s. What the customer wants…

And then, eventually, after the fish course, to the steak. I knew what was coming, but for the life of me I could not help myself. I do not normally go around the restaurant, leaving that to others, but clearly, I must have been possessed of some sort of masochist tendencies that evening.

"Major, and how are you and your family enjoying your meal?" I asked as I casually sauntered by, hoping not to have to break my stride. I felt, just at that moment, a bit like Basil Fawlty.

Why did I do that? I knew that I was walking right into it.

"Well, since you ask, this is quite the toughest steak that I have ever had the misfortune to have placed before me."

I knew it, I just knew it. Those words were almost verbatim to the ones he used every single time he ordered steak, which he did on every single occasion that he had been a customer.

At my shoulder, their young waitress Poppy, a local lady with some delusions of grandeur of her own because she and her husband had recently purchased their council house, looked down her nose, and was about to say something which would certainly have inflamed things. I jumped in before she had a chance, but not before the Major's stentorian tones had carried right across every table in the room – as he had very well intended. People looked up, startled. Knives and forks clattered down on to expensive china. Mouths dropped agape. Heads turned. Wine glasses, held aloft, quivered.

Time to defuse the situation before it got out of hand.

"May we prepare another one for you, Major?" I said in what I hoped were hushed tones that would not reach the other diners. I really was feeling more and more like Basil Fawlty.

"No. God knows where you get it from. The next one will be just the same, probably."

"Well, Major, it pains me to point out that we have had this conversation a number of times before..." I hesitated a moment and decided to get it off my chest for the first time. "You are a regular customer here, and for that we are, of course, most grateful. Every time you visit us you order steak, well done, and manage to eat most of it. Every time, without exception, you use those same words to describe it. What more can I do? Of course, there will be no charge for your own meal."

A fleeting smile broke out across his ruddy weather-beaten features. The Major had got what he wanted all along, and I had lost the price of a fillet steak. Not a score draw, I thought, but quite a lot in my favour with two other meals, wines, drinks and coffee. I knew full well that his wife bought their steak from the very same village butcher's shop that supplied us at that time.

The next time I was in the village centre, I popped into the butcher's shop.

"You know the old Major – well, of course you do, don't you, Colin?"

"Mmm, yes, only too well, said Colin. "A right old curmudgeon he is, between you and me."

"Well, he gets his steak here, doesn't he?"

"Yes, true, but I have actually been thinking of telling him to go elsewhere."

"Oh! Why?" I queried.

"Well, he never stops complaining and I'm sick of it. And to make it worse, he seems to deliberately speak louder in front of other customers, and I'm getting a bit of adverse reaction to it all."

"He does exactly that with me, too." I responded wryly. "Good luck".

Chapter 15

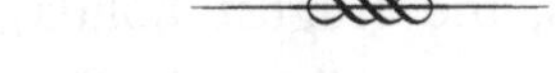

Disgruntled Hotelkeepers

Everyone who goes to stay at an hotel has the right to expect that their bathroom, in particular, will be pristine. Sometimes, however, guests seem to believe that pristine should mean never having been used before, which is obviously seldom the case. It is not easy, actually, to keep bathrooms in that sort of condition, even the latest ones with all the bells and whistles incorporated. Water, limescale, mould and guests are the four major problems, and of those four, the guests always win hands down for being the most trouble.

Our chambermaids were equipped with Milton cleaning fluid and toothbrushes to scrub away at the first sign of mould creeping on to tile grouting, but I have lost track of the number of things that guests have broken over the years. Pull cords get ripped from their sockets, water floods everywhere, tiles are cracked or chipped, and (quite how they do it) large chunks of enamel come off baths and basins. I can only conclude that most people in their own homes have cracked wash hand basins, if the number that I have had to change over the years is anything to go by. Most lotions and potions come in plastic bottles, so what on earth do people take on holiday with them that has the strength to crack a wash handbasin or chip a bath?

In the early days, the August holidays meant that families or couples booked well in advance to stay for the regulation fortnight and were wonderful for business. The summer would become fully booked quite early on, with no suggestion from either side to request or offer anything based on that crude word "discount". How things changed, and not necessarily for the better.

Nowadays, people want a discount at the drop of a hat.

Can their children go free? Why do they ask that? Why should they expect to go free? Do they expect them to be free at home? Will we not be expected to feed them, and clear up after them? We had always prided ourselves on being child friendly, although the type of premises did not lend itself to very small children. Most that came to us were little paragons of virtue, perfectly behaved and a pleasure to see around the place, bringing a welcome youthfulness to family gatherings. Inevitably there were exceptions, where parents appeared to abrogate all responsibility for their offspring the moment that they arrived.

"Go and have a look around while we unpack," or "Come and find us in the bar," were a couple of regular offerings.

The little blighters would then cause endless problems, dropping sticky things on carpets and trampling things down in the formal garden that had taken seasons to grow. And as for putting spilt drinks down on to tables…

And August people, as many would agree in our business, are nowadays the worst of all. They just don't seem to care at all. The building takes a hammering, and they help themselves to an over-abundance of breakfast, various fruits and buns being unashamedly crammed into pockets to be used later either to "feed the ducks" or themselves for a "free" picnic lunch. They do not even seek to hide the fact that they are taking more than they should.

Nor can you ever have enough hot water. There is nothing worse for a hotel owner than an irate guest complaining that there is no hot water for a bath or shower. This was a problem that I had to face on many occasions in the early years. Each time we had added on a new en-suite bathroom, we forgot that the inevitable result would be more hot water usage. I suppose we didn't realise that one day, the hotel might, joy of joys, actually be full.

All that new piping, and a dependency on three, admittedly large, electric water cisterns. They had huge rod-shaped elements sticking into their innards. We took to keeping a couple of those rods in our store, because to order them took a couple of weeks or so. But even with them to hand, we were at the mercy of a friendly electrician to fit them, and, to do so, the entire cistern had to be drained, then refilled, and of course, heated up all over again.

It all had to go, it really did.

New cisterns, spread around the attic areas, became the order of the day. There is only so much flak one can take from irate colonels bellowing down the telephone line that the *memsahib* was reduced to taking a freezing shower in February. Even worse when, just the once, the Colonel presented himself at the front desk, dripping wet, clad only in a towel that scarcely covered his girth and modesty. Was it done on purpose? We shall never know, but it had the desired effect. Carol took the brunt of that one, but it took her a couple of days to get over it!

All hotels also suffer from a degree of pilferage. I understand that the problem is even worse in supermarkets, where prices are actually geared to reflect what is euphemistically known as "shrinkage".

I had reached the conclusion over a couple of years that our French guests must be suffering from a shortage of high thread-count sheets in their home country after sheets started to disappear, giving a whole new meaning to the phrase 'French nickers'. It is pretty easy to identify who is to blame when your chambermaids go into a bedroom to make up the beds after guests have gone, only to find that the top sheet is missing. I was so pleased that we hired our sheets and pillow cases from a local laundry, instead of owning them outright. Guests wreck sheets. And we would have had to pay if we had not carried "surplus" stock.

Towels, too, were always an easy target, and not just for our French guests. We had particularly nice large ones, always fluffy as one would like to have at home. Inevitably, they were a target and a supply had to be kept in our stock to replace those that mysteriously found their way into departing guests' suitcases.

Call it ignorance or naivety, but theft was not something that had really occurred to me until I walked through the hall one day and found, to my surprise, a nail protruding from the wall, with nothing hanging on it. I stood and stared, not believing the evidence of my own eyes.

I called together everyone on duty and pointed out the nail.

"How long do you reckon that the painting has been missing?" Nobody had any comments, and nobody looked in the least guilty, to me at any rate. I wondered just how long we had all been walking past a nail that was no longer supporting a small oil painting of a bunch of flowers in a vase. It was a nice enough painting, though I had no idea as to whether it had any particular value.

It remained a mystery. But the next thing to go was a rather lovely stick barometer that also hung in the hall. Closely followed by a nest of silver swan ash trays.

There was a small saleroom in the next village, and a coterie of buyers would use our premises for breakfast, coffee or a quick lunch when there was a sale on. Possibly unfairly, I put two and two together and decided on four being an unscrupulous dealer. What could I do? Nothing.

Even more outlandish was the attempted removal of a television from one of our bedrooms. It was not long after we had installed remote-controlled colour TVs into each bedroom, and I suppose that they were still something of a novelty for some. A nice couple – well, I had thought them to be a nice couple – had been staying with us for the weekend. Come departure day, they were slowly bringing their stuff down the stairs and packing it into their motor car. They had refused our offer of moving their cases for them. The chap appeared at the top of the stairs with a large brown cardboard box, just as I was leaving the reception area, and we almost bumped in to each other.

"What have you got in there, then?" I said jokingly. "The crown jewels?"

He just looked shifty, and went so bright red that I knew something was amiss. He put the box down and didn't quite say "It's a fair cop, Guv" but he did say something like it. I opened the top of the box and there was a colour TV of identical size and make to the ones that we had installed in our bedrooms. I found, when I went to look in the room, that it was singularly lacking a TV.

He lugged it back upstairs and reconnected it. I, rather stupidly in hindsight, told him to get off the premises and not to come back, and did not report him to the police.

The cheek of it, in broad daylight, too, trying to nick a telly!

But perhaps the daftest theft of all that comes to mind was the incident of the bacon. Some staff see it as their right to pop a half pound of butter or something similar into their coat pocket when they finish their shift. Small items are forever going adrift in hotels.

One day, we ran out of back bacon. I was rather surprised about that, as we had a decent stock control system in place. It was at a time when we were buying our bacon from a particular supplier to the trade, and the large catering packs were marked accordingly. I was due to go to the wholesalers the next day and so I mentioned to our then breakfast cook that she would have to do without any back bacon for 24 hours.

"Don't you worry, sir. I've some in my freezer, and I'll bring it with me in the morning to save you going out. It will defrost overnight."

As you may guess, I was very grateful, and I said so.

Imagine my consternation therefore, when a brand-new catering pack of bacon, stamped with my wholesalers' moniker, was brought in by the cook. She was completely unaware of the giveaway stamped on the back of the pack and thought that she was doing me a big favour in bringing back my own bacon to me. It gave a whole new meaning to the phrase "bringing home the bacon". She could not have got it anywhere else other than our stores, to which she later admitted. She left us quite soon afterwards, but at my convenience once I had found a replacement.

After another busy summer, Sally and I took ourselves off for a couple of nights to a country house hotel in the Yorkshire Dales as a treat for Midge and Moss, though it was to be as much fun for ourselves. We love the Dales; all those rolling hills bisected by dry stone walls, and with clear rippling streams crackling over rocks along the valley floor. I have heard it referred to as "God's own country" but surely that must be a mistake, for otherwise, why would God have invented the Peak District?

The main reason for choosing that particular hotel was that we had learned they welcomed dogs, and they were in superb walking country. After a lengthy drive through wonderful scenery, punctuated by a number of stops for animal relief purposes, we drew up in front of a lovely black and white painted property, complete with a tinkling steam running through the grounds. It was picture perfect.

In the porch were racks of well-used wellies, fortunately very few of them being of the designer variety. Muddy and well-worn hiking boots took up all of one side of the entrance. A promising start...

After a brisk no-nonsense check-in, we took our case up to our room. Our bedroom featured a four-poster bed and it was with difficulty that we explained to Moss and Midge that it was to be off limits to anything with more than two legs.

After unpacking quickly, it was time to stretch those doggy legs around the village, stopping for smelling duty at each kerbside tree. As there were no lamp posts to be seen, it was going to get jolly dark later on the way back to the hotel. A vast trencherman's dinner was taken in the centre of the village at the one and only hostelry, with some succulent morsels being surreptitiously passed beneath the table towards pleading eyes, followed by a quick trip around the block; and then back to the hotel and that four-poster bed and doggy beds respectively.

The early wake-up call was not just the sun streaming through the rather thin curtains (I have a theory about that – hotels want you to wake up early so that the staff can get into your room that much the sooner) but by the arrival in our faces of cold wet noses and moist tongues.

We pulled on our walking gear and went down for breakfast. I moved towards the front door to put the dogs out in the car.

"Where are you off to, so early, then?" said the waitress.

"I'm just going to pop them in the car so that we can have our breakfast. You won't want them in the dining room."

"No, that's true, but come on through to the lounge and I'll set you up a small table, and you can all be together." I thought that to be a very kind offer, and we moved through to the lounge, where we saw a family finishing their breakfast, their Cocker sitting obediently at their feet. With a friendly nod to us, they put down their napkins and departed for their day out.

Having placed our order, we started on the tea and coffee, and that is when the highlight of the stay became apparent.

Our two full English breakfasts were laid before us – more than enough to keep us going through some hard morning walking. But, blow me down, then appeared two further full breakfasts, minus the tomato, perfectly served and presented, which were laid down on a rubber mat for our dogs. We were speechless!

"Don't worry! This is something that we do for all of our dog owners that come to stay. They need a good stomach full where you will no doubt be off to with them. Enjoy, woofers!" and with that she toddled off, by which time a certain two plates had already almost been licked clean.

Quite a place, that, and so we became regular visitors, despite the distance.

Although hotel inspectors are a necessary evil, I had the greatest admiration for them, particularly those from the AA. As for most of the others, well, it was more a case of offering tea and biscuits, and then making it all up as one went along.

I became very canny in spotting hotel inspectors. As we rose through the ranks, we received a lot of attention from them. As well as those from the AA and the RAC, there were numerous others to be on the lookout for. The list would eventually include, in no particular order, Johansens, Ashley Courtenay, the local tourist board, Michelin, Relais Routiers, Best Loved Hotels of the World, Egon Ronay, Signpost and the odd consortium. You could cover your front entrance with plaques displaying stars or other symbols should you so wish. We were a bit selective in that matter, and we occasionally had an inspector complain that we were not displaying their in-house identification.

Some inspectors even made an advance appointment, revealing their identity, to be sure of my being there when they visited. With that type of guidebook one could virtually write one's own entry, which to my mind made the whole exercise worthless for the general public who might buy the guide. But buy them they did, and doubtless as a result of my flowery prose, they came along in droves.

That was only the minority, of course, as most guide inspectors played by the rule book and were made of much sterner stuff. That's why I needed to know who they were.

I had a reasonable memory for faces and voices, and so when AA inspectors called for a reservation, I would often know who they were and when they arrived, I greeted them professionally, without displaying the slightest hint of recognition. After a further couple of years had passed, Mr F just said who he was when the reservation was made, and I would grin at him and shake hands as a regular customer on his arrival. Mind you, Mr F never went easy on me. The AA always had a firm approach and were very professional. I used them quite a bit for free advice. It seemed to me to be rather sensible to take them into my confidence about room upgrades or the like. They were far more likely to have an ear close to the ground about future movements and requirements, so I happily rode on the back of their expertise, and Mr F was a great help to me.

I think that the AA appreciated it too, because one year, after an annual inspection, I received a hint in which the words "Red Stars" were quietly mentioned. For those not in the know, to have AA Red Stars is the holy grail within the hotel industry. A lot of people will only stay at Red Star hotels, and they expect to pay that much more for the privilege.

I was all of a lather and every member of staff received a pep talk and a discussion about exactly what their job involved (as if they didn't know that already) and what an inspector might be on the lookout for in this particular instance, should we be lucky enough to be inspected on that basis.

We did indeed receive such an inspection some months later. The inspector, who was about the only one that I never sussed out, was in fact the chief inspector of the AA who at that time always operated anonymously, as I well knew. He arrived in good time for dinner and had a pot of tea in the lounge beforehand. He wore a suit and tie for dinner, and I put him down as just another businessman.

He came down after breakfast, trundling his overnight bag on wheels and paid his bill. Then he handed me his business card. The penny dropped and I tottered into the lounge with him. The meeting was mercifully brief. After the usual introductions and platitudes on both sides, he let me down gently.

"The wardrobe in my bedroom. Quite a lot of dust on the top of it. It hasn't been dusted recently."

There was nothing to say. I chewed that one over in silence. I knew that I had spoken to the chambermaids about that very issue. It turned out in this instance that the chambermaid was quite short (and clearly a bit lazy to boot) and the wardrobe was antique and rather tall.

"I will say that you have a very nice hotel here, and my meal last night was exemplary." It was cold comfort to my ears.

He went on, after a brief pause, "You might consider that you could be better served by applying for another AA star instead of staying at this level with Red Stars." I knew just what he meant. Thinking commercially, our type of business could prosper better, in his opinion, in the mainstream rather than within the absolute exclusivity of the much-prized Red Stars.

I took the hint, and we parted amicably. In its own way, it was a bit of an accolade for us for the chief inspector of the AA to make nice remarks about his stay in general and to actually visit us in particular. I waved him on his way and then took the rest of the morning off, lest I say something to that chambermaid that I might later regret. Carol, I believe, took her to one side and whispered in her ear.

My flirtation with Red Stars was well and truly over.

They were not to be part of my niche marketplace, and in hindsight, rightly so.

Some of the inspectors of slightly lesser organisations were not directly employed and presumably worked on some sort of commission basis. Those were the ones where you could literally write up your own entry into their so-called guides. A good friend of mine couldn't gain an entry to one of those annual guide books for love nor money and so in some desperation he enlisted my help. I asked him what had happened when he had been inspected. It did seem very odd to me, because all of these guides exist by making money from entries, and our dear friend Peter had a very nice inn which would have suited that guide perfectly. I asked him what had happened so far when he had been inspected.

"Well," he started indignantly, "I rang them up and asked what I had to do to join. They told me to fill in a form and then they would send someone round to meet with me and do an inspection."

OK, so far, so good. Perfectly normal procedure, as I assured Peter.

Waving his arms around, he spluttered, "Then, one day, a week or so later, this pretentious pompous ass turned up on my doorstep. He arrived in an old white Roller."

"What, a Rolls Royce?"

"Yes, it looked like an old wedding cake, well past its sell by date!"

Peter is not the most tactful of persons, and I could

almost see his hackles going up before we got to the nub of it.

"He parked right outside the front entrance, almost blocking it. Then he barged in through the front door and waved his card in my face."

"Well, just OK so far… and then…?"

"I've come to judge you!" he shouted across the hallway, to the consternation of a number of guests who had just finished their lunch. Wrong choice of words, although I did get the impression that perhaps the two had met locally before.

Peter told me that he jumped up, scuttled out of his office, and shouted back at him: "Only God can judge me, so buzz off out of here!!"

Not quite the response that you should expect from a seasoned hotelier, but Peter has ever been a touch excitable. The poor inspector beat a hasty retreat, and even my direct plea to the managing director of that guide would only evermore fall on deaf ears.

Over the years, as Nigel gradually started to ail, quite coincidentally I was introduced to a young lady by the name of Linda. She was a professional gardener already looking after a number of properties. She and Nigel worked together for a while, with her gradually taking on more and more. She took over doing the whole of my garden at the cottage, and I spent a lot of time playing truant, chatting away with her. She would clip and prune when I was mowing the lawn, weaving in and out of the fruit trees on Nigel's ride-on mower. How come he could always handle it so deftly, cutting right to the edge of a tree or bush, whilst I, on the other hand, was a complete butterfingers, and would, as soon as not, chop some bush to smithereens?

Carol, Reg, Nigel and Linda were a great help to me in keeping my life on an even balance in difficult times, and I drew great comfort from each and every one of them, pleased that I could make time – often too much – to spend in their company. I am greatly beholden to them all.

But, eventually, Nigel was no more. His wife rang to say that he would not be coming for a while and that he had fallen sick. Her next telephone call, mercifully soon thereafter, was to say that he had passed away.

I went to his funeral, held in a tiny church on the estate of the local squire, where I had known that Nigel had worked for most of his life before he came to me. Special permission was granted for him to be buried there in the "family" churchyard. It just tipped it down on the day. When I arrived at the little church on the grand estate, I could find nowhere to park my car within reasonable distance, there was so much mourner traffic. It was by then standing room only at the church; I, along with a lot of others, had to stand outside, soon drenched to the skin. There must have been over a hundred people there; a magnificent tribute to a true gentleman and countryman that I was proud to have known and been able to call my friend.

Chapter 16

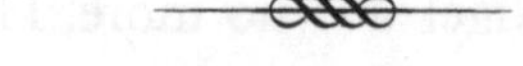

Bowing Out

The hotel was now humming along like the proverbial Swiss watch, as my good friend had kindly said. I had been so lucky to have accumulated a core of superb staff around me, and I could leave the day to day running in the capable hands of Carol, who had blossomed during her time with us. Everywhere was spick and span, up together, and, as far as I could see, the restaurant was on course to be awarded yet another consecutive year of 2 AA Rosettes. My oldest Border terrier, Midge, had entered her old age a while back, and I could see that Moss was moving on that way. Neither now needed the sort of exercise that they had lapped up in the past. Physically and mentally, I too was grinding slowly to a halt – or at least slowing down, burnt out from the efforts of all that had gone before over so many years.

One fine day, in late morning, I collapsed in my cottage. I don't know how long I was "out of it" for, but when I came around to my senses, I felt desperately ill and only just managed to totter across the lane and into the hotel. Through the front door I stumbled, left it open to the four winds, and fell over into the first chair that I came to. Only half conscious, I recall somebody saying, "He does look ill; he's gone all grey."

"I'm going to dial 999!" said Carol, whilst almost simultaneously throwing a blanket or rug over me. Mercifully, an ambulance arrived very promptly. I was loaded on to a trolley and bundled into the back and after an assessment, which I thought would take for ever, we sped off to the hospital where I was rushed straight to the cardiac ward and hooked up to a vast array of monitors and wired up to an ECG. The readings told the doctors that I had not had a heart attack, but that I was suffering the results of acute stress and other related problems.

Sally had been told about it, and Marcus too, so they were quickly at my bedside. By the time that my ex-wife arrived – who had told her? – I was sitting up and feeling perkier. Three days later, after many more tests, I was driven back home by Sally and told to rest.

Carol, as I had expected, had risen to the occasion, lived in at the hotel, and kept the ship on an even keel. I cannot thank her enough.

They do say, though, that it never rains but it pours. A month or two later, halfway through the morning we had to call the ambulance once more. This time, it was for my mother.

Getting well on in years and on the cusp of moving from the autumn to the winter of her life, she suffered a stroke. A terrible wail emanated from her and, rushing to see her,

I could see that she displayed all the classic symptoms. Her doctor came immediately and, to his eternal shame, pronounced it a minor TIA and that she would recover in due course. Even I could see that was wrong, and I told him that if he did not call for the ambulance on the spot, then I would. After some persuasion, he did so, and my mother was lifted out of the hotel and taken to a specialist stroke unit at a hospital a way distant. I followed on behind, but, when she was settled in, I am not sure that she knew who I was, and it was very saddening.

She made progress as the days went by and the treatments kicked in, and lucidity returned, though not the use of her legs. My mother had fought when her surgeons had said that she would not walk again after her car crash all those years ago, and that indomitable spirit would serve her well again. She would not walk other than for a few frail steps, but she battled on, displaying what I can only describe as that World War Two spirit that had served her and so many others.

The fright that I had received brought it home to me that my time had surely come and that it was a clear signal to look to release the helm at the hotel. I fought it, of course, because I could never see myself without it; it had become an integral part of my life, the tapestry that I had woven around myself and that building over so many years would link us for ever.

Oh, how I tossed and turned. Was my time really up at the hotel? Had the moment come, at last, to sell? To move on to pastures new? I found that I was thinking almost every day about finding an easier life, needing a let up from the relentless urgency to stay on top of my game.

I believed that I had done my best, all that I could, and I came to accept that I had taken the hotel as far as I was able in terms of my own vision, honed over all those long and often tumultuous years. Of course, others would have different visions and my grand old lady would start anew on another course on her journey – but not with me, I concluded.

It was a moment of ineffable sadness when I finally took the difficult decision to sell and move on. But somewhere in the background was an immediate lightening of the heart and a time for joy, albeit rather muted. I knew inside me that the time was ripe for my departure. I was in danger of becoming completely burned out, and a new life with hopefully a new wife beckoned, though I had no idea at that stage where our life together would lead us.

And so, it came to the practicalities of a sale. Which agent should I use? What should I say to the staff? How long would it all take?

I fondly imagined that potential new owners would congregate in a queue and bid up the process, so keen would they be to acquire such a treasure.

To do the selling, I chose an agency with a high national profile that used glossy pictures and, it turned out, drove fancy cars. After the first flurry of interest, I heard nothing from them for a few weeks, and there were no more prospects sent around to view. I supposed it was not surprising in view of the dire economic climate at the time. I telephoned their offices and there was no reply. I tried again, and again, always with the same result. The penny finally dropped – they had gone bust!

So, I went to the big hitters, Robert Barry & Co., whose fees were a lot more, but, true to their reputation, they sent along a steady stream of prospective buyers. Most were from other groups or consortia, seeking to add to their portfolios. For some reason or other we did not fit in with what they were looking for. I put it down to the fact that I owned one of the most idiosyncratic hotel businesses that I had come across. It would take major changes to make my business conform to any corporate strategy. And I guess we were just that bit too small to fit in either.

But Robert Barry & Co. continued to tap the well of their prospective purchasers, and almost a year after I put the hotel on the market, along came a couple who actually wanted to buy.

Those people had never run an hotel before; he came from a completely different business background. She, meanwhile, gave the impression that she would not be getting involved much with the hotel, should they decide to buy. I never understood exactly what drew them to us.

On the day of their first visit, which I had timed for mid-afternoon as being the quietest period of our working day, I was on hand to show them round. They did a bit of a walk around and asked a few questions, all of which I was easily able to answer. I showed them a bedroom or two, but by no means did they ask to see them all. It was more a case of me showing them what I wanted them to see and leaving out parts that were, shall we say, less flattering. In all, they probably saw over about a third of the property. I don't remember them visiting the kitchens at all.

In hindsight, with their lack of hotel knowledge, they may not have known the right questions to ask – but that is why you should retain a professional adviser. I introduced them to Carol, who, I had made sure, was the only staff member in on my secret.

Then they poked around briefly in my cottage over the road, which was included as an option in the sale; I didn't really want to continue to live next door to my hotel after it had been taken under new ownership. I did love that cottage and its wonderful garden, complete with a selection of fruit trees at the far end and stunning views across the big field and down to the river. The only thing that I mentioned about the cottage to those purchasers was that I had extended the tiny kitchen to about double the size and put an en-suite bathroom above it. I don't think that they even went upstairs or walked around the garden.

I decided that this was not the moment to tell them about the resident ghost.

I hadn't seen that ghost myself, except for its appearance on the cover of a well-known national ladies' magazine, which someone, completely agog, brought into the hotel one day for me to look at. There, on that cover, was an old black and white picture of my little cottage, probably taken over 100 years previously, and standing in front of it in the porch was the faint image of the aforesaid ghost. Had it been superimposed? I never found out, though I had to assume so. But the article inside had been written by an historian of some note, and within the article were mentioned a number of forenames of previous owners or inhabitants – specifically mine, that of my mother, my aunt and even that of my then wife! I am not a great believer in coincidences such as that so I didn't sleep well for the next few nights. I still have that magazine picture and article and scratch my head over it.

Anyway, I wondered if I would ever hear from those prospective purchasers again, but within a couple of days I received a letter stating that, without the couple even looking over the hotel fully, or having it properly surveyed, the agents had received an offer – and at the full asking price. What could I say, other than – yes!

A non-refundable deposit was paid in due course, once both sides had appointed leeches – sorry, lawyers. A timetable was agreed. They were in a big hurry to complete, and suggested, literally, a fortnight. I had my doubts that such a timescale would even be feasible, bearing in mind the number of people that would have to be involved. I asked for written confirmation that the staff would be kept on for at least a minimum period – they had all been good to me, and I wanted to do my best for them. Once the contract had been signed, I called everyone together and informed them that I was selling up, and that the new owners, a private couple, wanted them to stay on, and had agreed in writing to do so.

That's the moment when people get jumpy and start to look around elsewhere. I was so lucky that everyone agreed to stay. If Carol or the head chef or one or two other key people had done a flit, life would have suddenly become very complicated.

Carol and the head chef sat down with me one afternoon after lunch service was over.

"Well, you kept that close to your chest, I must say!" said the chef.

"I'm so sorry," I told him, "but what was I to do? You've worked in other hotels, so you know the score. If I had gone public before anything was fixed, all sorts of rumours would have started flying about and before you knew it not only would all the village have known, but rumours might put off a purchaser, and I could quickly have ended up with no staff."

"So, we are both safe here, then?" That was his next question.

"Yes, you are. No question, they have agreed in writing to keep you all on, on the same terms."

Of course, there was nothing to stop them going if they wanted, so I hoped to clinch the deal by adding: "If you do stay on until the sale is complete and my departure, I agree to pay you both a bonus on the day that I go. Will you be happy with that? And is there anyone else that you think that I should try to tie in likewise?"

We mulled it over, and a few other key staff were included into my little scheme.

Finally, and all too soon, the big day arrived. My feet had not touched the ground for the last couple of weeks as I struggled to get everything done to ensure a smooth transition into new ownership. There was so much to do, so many people to consult and notify. So many suppliers to sign off. I really couldn't have done it without Sally and Marcus, who took time away from their jobs to mastermind my final exit.

A firm of stock-takers, employed by the incoming proprietors, checked every single bottle, every cabbage, and anything else that they could find and indeed everything else on the premises that was not nailed down, so as to produce a final figure for the stock. Without exception, I can state that they were the rudest and most unsavoury bunch of London people that I have ever had the misfortune to deal with. Eventually, a figure was agreed, accepted on both sides, signed for, and I took great pleasure as I then threw them off the premises.

Sally and I had gone to huge lengths to prepare a complete inventory of every single item within the hotel, whether it was a large freestanding mahogany wardrobe or a fork in the restaurant. Nothing was left out, other than some items of a personal or sentimental nature. Both sides held a master copy through their lawyers, though to my certain knowledge, the incoming purchasers never checked it through before taking over.

Early on the day of completion, two extremely large pantechnicons had drawn up and parked outside, blocking the driveway. They were laden with stuff for the new owners. I sent them off to park further away, as the time for handover of keys (and the money) was not yet due.

It didn't take long for inquisitive neighbours to "accidentally" bump in to me to enquire what was going on. Those large removals lorries had rather given the game away.

Standard time for such exchanges, I had been told, was usually noon. And so, just before the witching hour, I welcomed the buyers into the lounge and offered them coffee, or something stronger, followed by sandwiches. Fortunately, nobody but myself seemed to realise that it was they, not I, who were effectively by then paying for it all, lunch included, because it was after the stocktaking had been concluded. Sally and I delved in to a hearty meal as we sat down for a few minutes with Carol and the kitchen brigade.

The minutes ticked by. The telephone lay ominously silent. People came in and drifted into the coffee shop. By 1 p.m. both sides were shuffling feet and looking anywhere other than at each other. They put in yet another call to their solicitor who stated quite categorically that the money had been received into their client account, and that the full amount had been transferred over. I called my solicitor who was equally adamant that they had not yet been put in funds.

Everyone told everyone else, with forced smiles, that it was just some hiccup in the banking system.

By 2 p.m. things had advanced not one whit. The same calls were made all over again, and the result of each call was the same.

By 5 p.m. things had become extremely fraught.

"Look, old boy, we have those blinking great vans outside. Will you at least allow them to start unloading?" The barely polite request came through gritted teeth from the would-be purchasers.

"Well, without wishing to be rude, the answer has to be no. As of this moment in time, you have not paid, so you don't get the keys or access to the property. My solicitor is very firm on that point. Sorry, and all that."

"But this is ridiculous! We have paid the deposit, which has gone through. Surely you can trust us?"

I could see that I was in a very difficult position. "The big problem is twofold. Firstly, there is no money to enable you to complete the transaction, and secondly, the transaction is over five hours late from the agreed time, and your solicitor appears unable to get your money to us. So, again, the answer must be no. Do have another cup of tea whilst we wait."

"I'm sick of your bloody tea!" As relations went from very strained to a complete breakdown, I made sure not to point out that it was in fact his own tea.

I phoned my solicitor who again confirmed that they had not been put in funds, and he was extremely clear, yet again, that I was to do nothing to jeopardise my position by handing over any keys or the like.

Should I start to panic? I was beginning to think so.

Just after 6 p.m. there was a sudden flurry of activity. Their lawyer rang the purchasers to say that the money had been misapplied by their bankers to someone else's account completely, and that they couldn't get it back without the account holders' authority.

I got up and marched out back to the reception area. I told the staff to get on with their regular duties, on my authority, because it looked as though we would be trading as usual that night. The other side immediately said that I could not do that, and I pointed out that since their money was not yet forthcoming, it was still my hotel and that actually I could do as I pleased.

The money finally arrived in my solicitor's account later that evening and I handed over the symbolic keys to both properties. Things were very strained as we finally shook hands and took our leave. Every single member of staff lined up outside to wave me off, Carol heading the team.

Of the new owners, there was no sign.

Sally brought the car to the front door, and I jumped in. I waved quickly and we pulled out of the driveway and towards the main road before anyone other than Sally could see the tears in my eyes.

And all of a sudden, it was all over.

Chapter 17

Moving On

The new owners were determined to go it alone and immediately put their own stamp on the place. I am sure that I would have done the same if the positions had been reversed, though as the old saying goes, "If it ain't broke, don't fix it." I had told them that we ran a rather complicated type of operation, where business came to us on a regular basis from quite a number of different opportunities, changing with the seasons. They were not interested to know anything that I had to say. I had offered to stay on for a couple of weeks free of charge to them, my services included in the sale price. They did not want to take me up on it. Madness, I thought then, for people who had never been involved with the running of an hotel before.

Sadly, it transpired that dear Carol was the first to leave, after just four weeks. I think that perhaps she made the error of pointing out to her new bosses that we had always done something in a particular way, and so why try to change it before they had got their feet properly under the table. Everything was in an upheaval, and she decided that she really didn't want to be part of it any more. I couldn't blame her for that.

Their first big decision, I was told, was that they did not want to continue to take pets – almost always dogs – at the hotel, as they themselves didn't like them. So, bang went well over 10% of their annual revenue stream straight away.

Wooden trestle tables and pub benches appeared outside the front of the hotel. Who would be using them? Certainly not the clientele that we had fostered so diligently. And what on earth did all that look like, completely spoiling the magnificent frontage.

It only took a couple of years, and by then the jungle drums had informed me that those owners were gone. I was told that every recommendation in those prestigious guidebooks, garnered so assiduously by me over many years, had been withdrawn, and that was effectively that. So sad; I think that the place then changed hands about four times over the next ten years, most likely spiralling downwards at each change. Oh, how were the mighty fallen.

I watched, from time to time, but from afar. I could never bring myself to go back.

It was time to move on with our lives. The actual sale of the hotel had been a bruising encounter and it had left me exhausted, wrung out, and feeling very flat. Not even the thought of the influx of money into my bank account seemed able to cheer me up.

Sally and I moped around for a month or two, as I settled into Sally's old house in leafy Lytham in Lancashire. I explored the delightful little town, went for long walks along the seafront with my old dogs, and joined the local library. Retirement? No, I could not face it for a while yet. There was a great void in our lives, aching to be filled. We cast around for something to do. Taking up golf again didn't do it for either of us, though we tried.

And so, we bought a house together, right there overlooking the sea – or rather the Ribble estuary leading out into the Irish Sea. Built in 1896 and firmly Victorian in appearance, it had three storeys, a cellar below them, four bedrooms and four bathrooms as well as all the other stuff that one might expect. It had been turned into three flats, but we could see beyond all that new cheap panelling and recognise the innate beauty that lay concealed beneath. We set about returning it to its former glory as a family home. It took nearly a year to sort out, reinstating all of the period features, having new coving, architraves and skirtings made in the old style, and knocking through walls to find original doorways and reinstate the rooms that lay beyond. Miraculously, most of the original corbels remained.

Released from hotel life, I did acquire a new car. After my divorce, with the accompanying severe financial penalties, I had gone instantly from my 911 to a ten-year-old Toyota with a leaky sunroof and a million miles on the clock. It served me very well for a couple of years. That sunroof leaked at the slightest shower of rain, but it was a small price to pay for a cheap set of reliable wheels, all I really needed, and all that I could then afford. A year later came a second-hand diesel Peugeot 306, which on one momentous occasion I managed to fill with petrol, only to have it die on me a few miles later as I pulled off the M6 late at night, mercifully close to an all-night garage. Now, I got myself back into a 911 in metallic black with a green leather interior. That green leather caused a lot of raised eyebrows, but I loved it. I got my own back after a few years when it became time to sell, because a couple of dealers entered into a bidding frenzy, just because of that outrageous green interior, one of a very, very, few that Porsche had made and delivered in UK specification.

My mother had joined us in Lytham, though she was almost bedridden when I sold the hotel. She and Puss travelled in my car as we made the long journey, and it must have seemed a strange cavalcade, which took most of a day to complete, with many stops along the way. A year later, my mother's long and fruitful life ended, with Sally and me at her side, in a lovely nursing home. At the very end, she pressed my hand and said "John, I never knew that it would end this way." And with that, she was gone.

A while later, we invested in an apartment in a spanking new building in northern Tenerife, down in the Canary Islands. We had been to stay with an old friend – Peter of that renowned inn on Dartmoor – and fell for the area, which was far from the madding crowds, though close to all amenities, verdant and for the most part unspoiled unlike the huge holiday resorts of the south of the island. No wonder that Peter had moved there to live his life of retirement with his beloved standard poodles, Millie and Rosie.

We found ourselves going over there more and more, and we eventually decided to make the break and live there full time.

But there was by then a third member of our household to consider – some might say the most important member.

Young Freddie, a crossbreed Staffie/Jack Russell had been rescued by the RSPCA when he had been abandoned on the streets at the tender age of some 6 weeks old, far too soon to be taken from his mother. As a result, he had to be taught by us the simple things that his mother would have taught him, such as how to clean himself. We fell in love with that little bundle, totally and completely, and I queued, one freezing morning, for hours, to be sure of securing him once he had reached his release date. The first thing that he did, as he leapt towards me, was to relieve himself on one of my shoes. It was an instant bond, to be held between us for his lifetime.

Freddie was simply to transform our lives, uplift us, and enrich our later years. How he achieved that, taking joyously to a new life with us on a sub-tropical island, is recorded in my first book, *Dog Days in The Fortunate Islands*. I hope that you will enjoy reading of his exploits. Freddie stole our hearts like no other for twelve years, fulfilled our every waking moment and made our lives so much the richer. I am quite unashamed in my declared love for that dog – and he for us – he was simply the best of the best.

In the meantime, because I had been a hotelkeeper with an award-winning restaurant, I was asked by a Spanish newspaper to become their restaurant reviewer, or *Critico Gastronomico* as my business card so fulsomely announced. It was a happy association for five interesting years that led me to seek out some wonderful places well off the beaten track – and there are lots of those over there. Then, time to move on to pastures new, and reflect on where life had taken me since I became a reluctant hotelkeeper.

That old building had become an integral part of my life and I think that I came to know every brick of it intimately. The endless flow of people that came through my front door (despite a very few leaving sooner than they might have expected) has enriched my life and left Sally and me with enough fond memories to sit and recall in our dotage. If you think that such a life could be for you, think hard, gird up your loins, and then go for it!

Despite all the efforts burning me out, and the 35 years or so that it took me to get the place where I wanted it to be, I have no regrets. Despite my initial reluctance, I can now look back on the ups and downs of my time there with a great residue of love, not just for the grand old building, but for those who helped me to achieve my goals.

So, what now?

Well, a work colleague that I knew a long time ago once said to me, in answer to my question as to what he might do in the autumn of his years:

"I can think of nothing better than to sit on a sunny terrace with a glass of cold white wine, with my family nearby."

And with Sally by my side, yes indeed, that will do for me.

Acknowledgements

There are a number of people whom I wish to thank for their tireless efforts in supporting me through to the production of this, my third book. When I first put finger to keyboard, I really didn't comprehend that I knew nothing, absolutely nothing, about the writing and construction of a book. I was about to enter a different world. And so it has proved, right up to and including this latest one.

As well as writing, I am an avid reader, and do my best to write reviews. I even read the acknowledgements section of books, and am amazed at the number of people that form the support group for more eminent scribes than I. Some lists run to the naming of more than 30 people. What they do is often not clear to me, but they have obviously played an important part in the eyes of those writers and they are lucky to have such extensive support teams. My own support team is rather more modest.

Most importantly, I must thank my wife, Sally, who has read each draft, made suggestions and generally supported me through the process, mostly without complaint! Whilst I have enjoyed the process of writing immensely, it must have been a serious trial for her.

I had thought of writing out a list of staff that had helped me turn the hotel into what it became. I then thought that, should I have forgotten someone (old age has its drawbacks) I might offend that person. So, I am not going to put names on a list, but am content that, should you happen to read this, you will know who you are, and please accept my thanks and realise that I truly appreciated you all.

My long-suffering editor Jennifer Barclay has, as usual, been tireless in slicing huge swathes of useless verbiage from what I fondly imagined to be the finished product. She has not only shaped my book, she has improved and honed my writing and presentation, let alone my punctuation. Her skill has been greatly to my benefit, and, simply put, I could not have done all this without her. I said in my first book that I was so lucky to have met her, and I feel the same about her to this day. What she thinks of me, of course, may be entirely different!

My son and I have come through it well, despite a lot of ups and downs. He has stood beside me during difficult periods when I knew that I had no right to expect that of him, and for that I am humbled.

I am grateful to all the staff at Troubador Publishing who have worked so tirelessly to bring my book to print. Their help and advice along the way has been invaluable. The publisher, Jeremy Thompson, took my first manuscript home with him and read it in his garden over a weekend, before enthusiastically giving me the green light. Troubador have been publishers of all my books and it has been a pleasure to work with them.

My heartfelt thanks go out to you all.

The great majority of events in this book are true, although I have occasionally changed some names to protect anonymity and where so required, to protect reputations. The location of my old hotel has been disguised and shifted slightly to preserve anonymity for new owners. Some scenarios have been enhanced to provide a better flow, though they remain inherently true to life. My characters have been inspired by real people, mostly my friends, but occasionally quite the opposite, and I hope that they will excuse me if I have inadvertently exaggerated anything in my storytelling. Any errors are mine alone.

Front cover design and village map are by the very talented John Harding.

Find him at www.johnharding.net

Thank You!

Thank you for reading this book, which has been written partly in response to kind readers of my first book wanting to know about what I did before we moved to a new home in northern Tenerife. I hope that you have enjoyed the story of my life at the helm of what eventually turned out to be a rather nice hotel.

If you have enjoyed it, may I suggest that you try my first book – *Dog Days In The Fortunate Islands* – which tells the story of my retirement, with my wife and our dog, to begin a new and surprisingly exciting life in the Canary Islands. Told with humour and pathos, it is a light-hearted journey that I hope will enthral and amuse you in equal parts.

Writers need reviews; it is their oxygen. If you have enjoyed this book and if you have the time and inclination, please let me know what you thought. Even better, if you are able to write a short review – however brief – that would be wonderful. If you were then able to post it on to Amazon or your favourite book site, that would be wonderful. By doing that, you not only help out authors, but you help new readers to find us as well, which ultimately benefits everybody. Thanks in advance!

Please do visit me for my latest news through my website:

www.johnsearancke.com

You are also very welcome to email me directly, and I promise to respond to every contact

johnsearancke@hotmail.com

DOG DAYS IN THE FORTUNATE ISLANDS

Determined to leave a life at the grindstone in grimy and wet Lancashire as retirement beckons, John, his wife Sally and their beloved foundling Freddie, a Jack Russell/Staffie cross, embark on the journey of a lifetime to relocate and live on the sunny island of Tenerife in the Canary Isles.

Selling up, they make the move to the north of the island, that part almost unknown to the casual tourist – their very own hidden Tenerife, almost a world away from the much-maligned tourist trap of the south of the island. Life in the north is relaxed, and they are surrounded by stunning views on the beautiful northern coast, where their new home is set amidst orange groves and banana plantations, their garden alive with hibiscus, oleander and wild poinsettias, and from their balcony they can see the island's volcano, El Teide, capped by snow in winter. Best of all, the weather is fantastic, the temperature idyllic, the people so friendly, and the cost of living outrageously low.

We learn the idiosyncrasies of buying a new home and car on the island, sorting out the legalities and integrating into the local community, interspersed with the stories of doggy derring-do and new canine friends. With a trip all the way through mainland Spain in an old classic car, adventures in far-flung places and visits to many out of the way restaurants, the question remains – can they stand the pace of this tranquil island life?

PRUNES FOR BREAKFAST

Another WW2 memoir? Yes, indeed, and for a very good reason. It could not be told before, until personal papers and photographs were made available to the author. This is the story of my mother and father, told mostly from the side of my father, from the time of his calling up in early 1940 to his release from a prisoner of war camp in Germany in 1945, thence to return to England to try to pick up the pieces of his old life.

Nothing could ever be quite the same afterwards, but travel through those 5 years, learning of the ups and downs, the plots and counterplots, as my father rose through the ranks to end his war as a captain, elevated to that rank in the field as his troops faced the formidable might of the

SS Panzers, and where his battle came to an abrupt end, surrounded in an orchard by the enemy and captured after a series of bloody skirmishes as the British army spearheaded its way from the beaches and through the *bocage* of Normandy. Such was the fighting that a VC was won close by.

His journey across France and Germany in a truck, with comrades dying each day, is as hard to tell as it may be to read, particularly when a new life and new harsh rules had to be learned and rigidly enforced in a prison camp in Germany, his final destination. Not all was doom and gloom however, because who else would order a new car whilst in that German prison camp, so certain that he would be home in time to take delivery?

The story is full of uplifting moments and may possibly be the first time that an individual's war story has been told in such a homespun and ordinary manner, complete with extracts of letters that passed between husband and wife over those 5 long years, adding greatly to the poignancy of the telling of the tale.